A Working Man's Credo

A Working Man's Credo

Intimations on Immortality

Ross Johnson

McAvaney Media Pty Ltd
Adelaide, South Australia

Contents

Publishing detail

Ross Johnson © 2012
Published Adelaide, Australia, 2013.

office@mcavaney.com   www.mcavaneymedia.com

Poetry by John Pfitzner reprinted with kind permission of his family. His collection Fence Music *is published in* Friendly Street New Poets 17, *Wakefield Press, Adelaide, 2012.*

First Edit: John Pfitzner, Adelaide, 2011.
Layout, Second Edit: Anne Johnson, 2013

National Library of Australia CIP data
Title: A Working man's credo
ISBN: 9780987550408 (paperback)
ISBN: 9780987550415 (ebook)

Notes: Includes bibliographical references
Subjects: Johnson, Ross, 1933-/Essays/Working class men–Philosophical aspects/Meaning (Philosophy)/Conduct of life
Dewey Number: 158.1

1

Our birth is but a sleep and a forgetting
The Soul that rises with us, our life's Star
Hath had elsewhere its setting
And cometh from afar:
Not in entire forgetfulness
And not in utter nakedness
But trailing clouds of glory do we come
From God, who is our home
Heaven lies about us in our infancy!
Shades of the prison-house begin to close
Upon the growing Boy, ...

William Wordsworth
*Ode: Intimations of Immortality**

Unafraid and questioning minds are essential in the pursuit of truth. (Anon.)

...we [must] recognise not only the eternal Spirit as the inhabitant of the bodily mansion, the wearer of this mutable robe, but accept Matter of which it is made, as a fit and noble material out of which He weaves constantly His garbs, builds recurrently the unending series of His mansions.

Sri Aurobindo[1]
Life Divine, 1916

This is an ambitious undertaking which in the end I fear will come to naught as it may not reflect the sentiments which I set out to convey. In that case it will be destined for the wastepaper basket. What am I trying to convey? Perhaps encourage a sense of wonder and expose the empty certainties of religious fundamentalism and the rigidities of atheism.

Now in the twilight of my sojourn here on earth my hope is that someone may find these musings of interest. I set them out not as a definitive conclusion as there can be no definitive conclusion – it is all a mystery – but rather as a philosophical counterpart based on a physician's methodology. In arriving at a diagnosis the physician tabulates all the patient's symptoms, which are those complaints which he or she voices to the physician. Next, the physician thoroughly examines the patient, interpreting his findings according to known standards. For example: rebound tenderness on abdominal examination indicates peritoneal irritation, possibly peritonitis, either chemical or bacterial. Thus, a list of differential diagnoses is formulated. How does he proceed further? Maybe certain tests will yield helpful additional information, perhaps a blood test or an X-ray. Only when all the possible evidence is accumulated, only then does the physician eliminate those less likely diagnoses in favour of the most likely diagnosis and prescribe appropriate treatment or take surgical action.

To my shame it is only in the last decade that I have applied myself with discipline to an analysis of the multitude of theological questions and opinions to which one is subjected all one's life. In the prime of one's life, attitudes tend to be pragmatic. Situations arise and there is a fork in the road – take the left fork and the consequences are such and such – take the right fork and the consequences are perhaps more to one's liking, even though one could be hard put to justify one's decision on strict moral grounds if put to the ultimate test.

As a boy and a young man I was in a hurry. As a twelve or thirteen-year-old I had a strong conviction and an urge to join the Cooneyites[2], but the sacrifice and family consequences did not sit well with me so I declined, eventually drifting away. Nevertheless, guilt remained for some years, being particularly strong during my sojourn in New Zealand in 1958-9.

On becoming engaged and moving to Canada, my overriding conviction was to have a family direction

which was united, unlike the dysfunction I witnessed in my own parents' relationship all my life, which was predominantly religion based. I therefore took instruction in the Lutheran Church in Canada and joined the Church, again a pragmatic decision based on outcome rather than conviction. I went along with the doctrines even though I thought they smacked of superstition intertwined with tradition rather than logic and were too high church for my upbringing.

My own children were quick to pick up the discrepancy and in their adolescence pointed out the shortcomings in my lack of conviction in the Lutheran Church, telling me I went along with it 'because of Mum'. Well, at the time, I disagreed with them, but they were right. Life was full, was complicated, and I was forging a career, feeding mouths, and was not prepared to take on yet another challenge and rock the boat more than I needed.

Eventually, retirement came, but this challenge continued to nag at my conscience; a decade passed, and it is only in the last year or so that my integrity demanded that I leave the Lutheran Church and start again from scratch. All bets were off!

No threat to any public institution, it's only my own beliefs that I'm going to overhaul.[3]

Cogito ergo sum. **[I think, therefore I am.]**[4]

Descartes

During the fourth and fifth centuries Christianity became a confessional church, drawing a line in the sand between those who were the orthodox believers and destined for Heaven and those scattered groups who were heretics and destined for the other place. A 'them and us' mentality developed which is alive and well today. The Nicene Creed is a good example. The virgin birth, the miracles and the resurrection are not literal happenings and yet we are asked to confess them as though they were. A way out is available for those who have trouble with their beliefs and that is called *sacrificium intellectus* (so-called by German Lutheran theologian Rudolph Bultmann[5]); one is called upon to sacrifice one's intellect (and as a by-product one's integrity as well!) and make the confession anyway. Merit is obtained and everyone can go home happy! Faith is, after all, a contradiction of reason, so we are told. At what point is one's personal integrity at stake; to what extent am I prepared to lie to get to Heaven? Critical thinkers can never be satisfied with the consensus of a committee, and that is the real origin of confessions and creeds.

It is refreshing to read of the struggles endured by honest souls, even those in high office, such as the following confession by Richard Holloway, latterly Bishop of Edinburgh:

I have already referred to the shift in Christian history from poetry to packaging. The journey, from a movement that tried to follow the example of Jesus to an institution that hardened round a particular interpretation of his meaning, took hundreds of years to complete. The theological shorthand for the shift is called the evolution from the Jesus of History to the Christ of Faith, the move from the man of Nazareth who challenged us to action against principalities and powers to the Godman of Christian orthodoxy who demands our belief. It is the reverse of the Schweitzer journey from word to act, from theology to service. Wrong words have to be punished because they threaten the citadel of belief into which we have escaped from the cold winds of an empty universe.[6]

Holloway includes here an extract from the diary of King Edward VI, recorded 2 May 1550:

'Joan Bocher, otherwise called Joan of Kent, was burned for holding that Christ was not incarnate of the Virgin Mary, being condemned the year before but kept in hope of conversion; and on the 30th of April the Bishop of London and the Bishop of Ely were to persuade her. But she withstood them and reviled the preacher that preached at her death.'

That entry...measures the distance the Church travelled away from Jesus and is still travelling today. The Christian test became words, the right words, the saving words. The biggest of these saving words is Resurrection, the word that captures the foundational belief of organised Christianity.

And that Easter of my first crisis I could not put the Church's meaning upon it. Yet I had to. I had to get into the pulpit of my little church and read the stories of how he had been killed and placed in a tomb. And how they had rolled a stone in front of the tomb. And how, three days later – though the accounts vary – his disciples had come to the tomb and found it empty. And how he had appeared to them over a period of forty days. And how at the end of the forty days they had seen him ascend – literally – into the sky towards heaven. And it was my duty to tell them that this story was true. And not in a poetic sense – I was good at that – but in a factual sense. I couldn't do it.[7]

By the fourth century this so-called universal (catholic) church had developed a 'canon' of writings that their committee described as 'God-inspired Scripture'. They discredited the literature of their competitors as not genuine and 'heretical'. Some of the texts from the early competitors of orthodoxy (and repressed by the winners) reveal amazing religious diversity in the early period of Christian evolution. These include the Nag Hammadi Library, the Gospels of Thomas and Judas and other texts.

The big breakthrough came when the fourth-century Roman Emperor, Constantine, declared the 'orthodox' Christian church to be the State religion, and with this political stamp of approval came the consolidation of the political and religious influence of the Roman Church.

What follows in this extended essay is a review of the yearnings of homo sapiens from early times, and a summary of my credo in 2011 – this may well change in 2012! Extensive reading has been conducted, free discussions with like-minded people has taken place with an exchange of view points and a 'differential diagnosis' list formulated. My daughter Catherine has asked me to document my thoughts.

Religion is always an individual, personal thing. Every person must work out his own views of religion, and if he is sincere, God will not blame him, however it turns out. Every man's religious experience is valid for himself, for…it is not something to be argued about. But the story of an honest soul struggling with religious problems, told in a sincere

manner, will always be of benefit to other people.

Lin Yutang[8]

The Importance of Living, 1938

NOTES

1. Sri Aurobino (1872-1950) was an Indian
nationalist, freedom fighter, philosopher, yogi,
guru and poet. He joined the Indian movement
for freedom from British rule and for a
duration became one of its most important
leaders, before developing his own vision of
human progress and spiritual evolution. He
had previously spent two years at King's
College, Cambridge. This quote taken from
Biman Narayan Thakur, *Poetic plays of Sri
Aurobino,* online at books.google.com.au/
books?isbn=8172111819, p. 41.

2. Editor's note: the author's mother was a
member of the Cooneyites in South Australia.
In his essay *The Life and times of Myrtle*, he
describes his experience of the sect through his
mother's membership during the 1940: *They
refer to each other as 'the friends,' or 'brothers' and
'sisters'. Their church has no name as they believe
there is no other path to heaven beyond their
organisation. They refer to their belief group as
belonging to 'The Way,' a term used in the New*

*Testament...They have no churches but a group of
perhaps a dozen or 20 congregate twice a week in a
designated home of one of 'the saints'. On Sunday
morning or afternoon the local elder leads the
service after all are gathered together in silence in
say the dining room or sitting room where the
chairs are arranged in a circle. A hymn is sung
unaccompanied and then each in turn delivers a
prayer all with the same theme of thanking God,
nothing personal. Another hymn and then personal
testimonies, delivered by each in turn in a
random fashion where they choose any scriptural
passage and describe the effect it has had on them
in the previous week.*

3. Rene Descartes, Discourse on the method of
rightly using one's reason and of seeking truth
in the sciences, 1637, Part II paraphrased by
Edward Craig in Philosophy, Sterling
Publishing Company, New York, 2009, p. 112.
Online at books.google.com.au/
books?isbn=140276877X.
4. ibid., Part IV. Online at
http://www.gutenberg.org/ebooks/59.
5. Rudolph Bultmann (1884-1976), a professor
of New Testament at the University of
Marburg, believed it was a waste of time

arguing over the historical facts of the
NewTestament. He advocated
"demythologising" the New Testament,
believing that all that mattered for a Christian
was to believe that Jesus existed, lived a holy
life and died by crucifixion.
6. Richard Holloway, Leaving Alexandria, The
Text Publishing Co., Melbourne, 2012,
pp.155-156.
7. Lin Yutang, The Importance of living,
William Heinemann Ltd., London, 1938, p.
411.

2

Deus Absconditus

Ascending skywards
seemed a good move.
From above the clouds I reached down –
with unlimited power –
to whip up storms,
shake the earth,
take sides.

I was disturbed by Copernicus et al,
who moved Earth from the centre and then,
with their telescopes
pushed me out beyond the solar system,
among the stars.

Then Hubble, showing
Andromeda to be
a separate galaxy
outside the Milky Way,
thrust me into
intergalactic space
where I was
kept on the run

To the far reaches of the universe,
back to the Big Bang
where I tried to squeeze
into the first nanoseconds
but found there's nowhere to hide
in a singularity.

I had no choice;
I returned to earth.
And I'm happy here,
back where I began,
in the place where
myth and metaphor meet,
having power
only to persuade,
lodged on the edge
of the liminal,
in the place of possibility
at the point of connection,
hidden in the flow,
the process,
the becoming.

John Pfitzner

3

Evidence for the Big Bang

Where to start? A good place, it seems to me, would be to
start at the beginning, the real beginning. The following
is taken from John David Ebert's[1] interview with Brian
Swimme who wrote *The Universe Story from the Primor-
dial Flaring Forth to the Ecozoic Era* (Harper San Francisco,
1992). Brian Swimme is a mathematician by training but
is a practising cosmologist who seeks a larger, warmer,
more noble science story, and states that science should
not be merely a collection of facts but should be a stu-
dent's guide to a grand world view, including, where possible, meaning, purpose and value. He is at the forefront
of a new movement – The Universe Story – that inte-
grates Science and Spirituality. He states:

*The first piece of evidence occurred when Edwin Hubble con-
firmed Einstein's prediction that the universe was expanding.
When Hubble looked through the Hooker telescope he saw that
the other galaxies were moving away from our own galaxy,
the Milky Way, and that the further away they were, the faster
they were moving; in fact twice as fast. If you reverse this*

process of expansion, ultimately you end up at an initial point – what cosmologists call a singularity.

Second, scientists realised that there should be some evidence around for the Big Bang, in the form of cosmic radiation. A couple of scientists, Penzias and Wilson, in 1965, were work-ing on a completely different project, but kept picking up this annoying interference. At first they thought that roosting pigeons might be messing up their satellite signals with their droppings. They scraped a considerable amount of this 'inter-ference' from their equipment, but the hiss persisted. The tem-perature of the hiss at 2.7 degrees kelvin (2.7 degrees above absolute zero) was consistent with what cosmologists hypoth-esised the background radiation from the Big Bang would be. They had inadvertently discovered the best proof for the Big Bang, and won the Nobel Prize for their efforts.

Finally, the amount of hydrogen, lithium and helium we actu-ally find in the universe is consistent with what scientists have concluded would be the case in the Big Bang scenario.[2]

When Einstein[3] first looked through the Hooker tele-scope on top of Mount Wilson and saw for himself what Edwin Hubble had discovered from the Doppler effect[4] – that the universe was expanding – he was elated. Prior to Hubble's discovery, astronomers had convinced Einstein that his general theory of relativity – which stated that the universe must be either expanding or contracting – was wrong; the universe was stable, they said. In a move he later called the greatest blunder of his life, Einstein had changed his equations to accommodate their perceptions. Hubble's discovery proved that he had been correct all along. The universe as a whole was developing. It was going somewhere.

This was news. Darwin had established that evolution was occurring biologically, as described in the next section. Now it was irrefutable that the whole universe had been on an evolutionary path before organic life emerged.[5]

Is this evolution occurring at random? This would be hard to imagine without there being complete chaos in the universe. Universal evolution is occurring under defined and immutable laws of physics, many of which, I believe, are yet to be discovered. The system works, has for billions of years, and will continue to do so regardless of the direction homo sapiens wishes to follow.

Stephen Hawking discussed a remarkable possibility in *A Brief History of Time*[6]. He suggested that we might be living in an undulating, cyclical universe without beginning or end. If his theory is true, then the Big Bang happened when matter became so compacted that an enormous explosion had to take place. That explosion pushed matter out into space, forming an expanding universe as we know it. After a time, the forces of gravity will reverse the movement, and the universe will gradually be drawn back into almost infinite mass. Another Big Bang. Another expansion, then another contraction!

In his online article *Cosmic Time Machine*, Australian National University's Dr Tim Wetherell invites us to travel back in time 'about four and a half billion years':

...we would be able to see the early planets of the solar system beginning to form around the infant sun.

This was a time of massive and enormously violent impacts as forming planets swept debris and each other out of their orbital paths. It was around this time, scientists believe, that a body about the size of Mars smashed into the planet earth with such force that enough matter was ejected to create the Moon.

Over time, things settled down. Planets gradually found their present-day orbits and the frequency of major collisions declined. Then, around four billion years ago, just about the time life was beginning on Earth, something odd happened. The orbits of Jupiter and Saturn shifted slightly, which in turn perturbed Uranus and Neptune. The gravitational effects of this reshuffle extended out into the Oort Cloud – a halo of comets in the outer solar system.[7]

The absolute enormity of the cosmos is...gobsmacking! There are some hundred billion galaxies, each with, on average, one hundred billion stars. In all the galaxies, there are perhaps as many planets as stars, a total of ten billion trillion! What overpowering numbers, and how irrelevant does this make homo sapiens!

Galileo, in 1609, lent his support to the Copernican theory that the Earth rotated around the sun rather than the reverse, and this belief caused him to fall foul of the Catholic Church and resulted in him being confined to house arrest for the rest of his days. It was not until 1981, nearly 400 years later, that the Catholic Church was prepared to admit that they were at fault, at a conference on cosmology organised by the Jesuits. At the end of the conference the participants were granted an audience with the Pope, who stated that it was alright to study the evolution of the universe after the big bang, but no inquiry should be made into the big bang itself because that was the moment of Creation and therefore the work of God![8]

NOTES

1. American John David Ebert describes himself as a cultural critic and philosopher. His interview with Brian Swimme is published in *Twilight of the clockwork God: conversations on science and spirituality at the end of an age*, Council Oak Books, Tulsa,1999, Ch.1.

2. Reproduced in Bruce Sanguin's *Darwin, divinity and the dance of the cosmos: an ecological Christianity*, Wood Lake Publishing, Kelowna, pp. 99-100.

3. In the 1930s, Einstein, who was a capable violinist, was working on a sonata with Artur Schnabel, a virtuoso concert pianist, and was having trouble mastering a tricky cross-rhythm. Schnabel looked intently at the

world's most famous mathematician and said to him, 'The trouble with you, Albert, is that *you can't count!'* Apart from equations, Einstein's other great cause was Zionism. Although he was Jewish by descent, Einstein rejected the biblical idea of God. His support for the Zionist cause was duly recognised in 1952, when he was offered the presidency of Israel. He declined. 'Equations are more important to me,' he explained, 'because politics is for the present but an equation is something for eternity.'.

4. Stars moving away from us cause the frequency of the waves we receive to be lower, with their spectra shifted towards the red end of the spectrum.

5. Bruce Sanguin, op. cit, p. 82.

6. Stephen Hawking, *A Brief History of Time*, Bantam Books, New York, 1998.

7. Tim Wetherell, 3 May 2010, *Cosmic Time Machine,* Science Alert Australian & New Zealand at http://www.sciencealert.com.au/features/20100305-20915.html. Originally appearing in ScienceWise Magazine, Autumn 2010 at http://sciencewise.anu.edu.au/articles/moon%20rock.

8. Stephen Hawking, op. cit., p. 122.

4

Galileo's Telescope

It could be just a toy
Or the latest advance in military technology
But when he aims it at the heaven
The whole cosmos is shaken.
Earth begins to spin,
hurtling through space
in its race around the sun.
On the lunar surface,
mountains and valleys appear –
the heavenly bodies
no longer perfect and immutable.
Each planet assumes its rightful place
in its elliptical heliocentric orbit.
Jupiter acquires moons and Saturn rings.
The sun's face becomes spotted.
Stars retreat to unimaginable distances.
Wonders are revealed
more wonderful than those they displace
as old certainties crumble with
the authorities that supported them.
The universe starts divulging secrets
in the elegant poetry of mathematics.

People learn to measure, imagine,
experiment, observe
and a later generation
sends people to the moon,
where a space-suited astronaut
outside his lunar module,
drops a hammer and a feather together
and sees them hit the ground
simultaneously.

John Pfitzner

5
_____

The Time Conundrum

In conjunction with a consideration of the enormity of space must be the theological implications of the concepts of time. We grow up believing our observations that time is an absolute measurement. There is a future, a present and a past. Time is regular and moves in one direction.

Albert Einstein[1] made the cryptic comment, 'The only reason for time is so that everything doesn't happen at once'. He produced a revolution in physics. Nothing travels at or beyond the speed of light. It is possible to travel at 99.9 per cent the speed of light but no more. There is a cosmic speed limit. Special Relativity, fully worked out by Einstein in his middle twenties, is supported by every experiment devised to check it. As the speed of an object increases, time slows down – time is not an absolute. Atomic clocks carried in aeroplanes slow down a little compared to identical clocks on the ground. If one were to travel close to the speed of light one would hardly age at all by comparison with friends and relatives left back home. It follows that if one were to go on a twenty-five year journey at the speed of light and return home, one would find that the friends and relatives were twenty-five years older but the age of the traveller was virtually unchanged.

As Stephen Hawking observed:

Up until the beginning of the last century people believed in absolute time; all good clocks would agree on the time interval between two events. However, the discovery that the speed of light appeared the same to every observer, no matter how he was moving, led to the theory of relativity – and in that, one had to abandon the idea that there was a unique absolute time. Instead, each observer would have his own measure of time as recorded by a clock that he carried: clocks carried by different observers would not necessarily agree. Thus time became a more personal concept, relative to the observer who measured it. [2]

Light from the Sun takes eight minutes to travel the ninety-three million miles to earth. The sunlight is eight minutes old when we see it. The further away stars are from the earth, the longer it takes for the light from them to reach this planet. The nearest star after the Sun is Alpha Proxima and light from that star takes a little over four years to reach us. The Hubble Space Telescope is able to look more closely at areas of space and see back into time to see the birth of stars.

The corollary of the above also pertains. The light that left the Earth in 1066 is now (in 2011) 945 light years away. So positioning oneself in space 945 light years away and looking back at the Earth one would see the light from 1066. By focussing on Kent, one would see the Battle of Hastings. Of course a pretty good telescope would be necessary.

So what are the theological implications? To be realistic, we on this Earth are trapped in time and space. These are the parameters within which we move. However, we have shown that cosmic time is not absolute, as was Sir Isaac Newton's belief, but relative, as Einstein proved. It follows that the Spirit of the Universe is not bound by absolute time but is independent of it. To use the analogy of a piece of string and an observer, the piece of string could be divided into individual centuries and the outside observer could plug into any one of these centuries in real time at his whim.

This leaves the Spirit of the Universe in very much the same position in regard to time as is His position with the Cosmos, as is described later in this essay. He can be immanent (in real earth time) or transcendent (looking at time from the outside like a string) as He pleases.

The transcendent possibility, of course, introduces other problems on which to ponder. If the whole of time can be set out like a piece of string, then is the whole of history predetermined? Stephen Hawking deals with this problem in a lecture he gave at a Sigma Club seminar at the University of Cambridge in April, 1990.[3] The argument for preordination used to be that God was omnipotent and outside time, so God would know what was going to happen. This being so, how could we have any free will and, ipso facto, how can we be responsible for our actions?

Stephen Hawking comes to some conclusions:

...the ultimate objective test of whether an organism has free will would seem to be: Can one predict the behaviour of the organism? In the case of human beings, we are quite unable to use the fundamental laws to predict what people will do, for two reasons. First, we cannot solve the equations for the very large number of particles involved...[the human brain contains a hundred million billion billion particles – far too many for solving equations and making predictions!]

...So, as we cannot predict human behaviour, we may as well adopt the effective theory that humans are free agents who can choose what to do. It seems there are definite survival advantages to believing in free will and responsibility for one's actions. That means this belief should be reinforced by natural selection...

In summary: Is everything determined? The answer is yes, it is. But it might as well not be, because we can never know what is determined.[4]

It seems that this circumlocutory debate arrives at a dead end!

NOTES

> 1. Albert Einstein was not conventionally religious but nor was he an atheist. In his 1949 collection of essays, The world as I see it, he wrote: *The most beautiful and deepest experience*

*a man can have is the sense of the mysterious. It is
the underlying principle of religion as well as all
serious endeavour in art and science...To sense that
behind anything that can be experienced there is
something that our mind cannot grasp and whose
beauty and simplimity reaches us only indirectly
and as a feeble reflection, this is religiousness...To
me, it suffices to wonder at these secrets and to
attempt humbly to grasp with my mind a mere
image of the lofty structure of all that there is.*
2. Stephen Hawking, *A Brief history of time*,
Bantam Press, London, 1989, p. 122.
3. Stephen Hawking, *Is everything determined?*
lecture at The Sigma Club, University of
Cambridge, April, 1990.
4. A version of this lecture is reproduced in
Stephen Hawking, *Black holes and baby
universes and other essays,* Transworld
Publishers, London, 1993, pp. 127-29.

6

On 'The Origin of Species', 1859

**We are co-creators with the divine in the evolution-
ary process.**
Professor Darren J. N. Middleton

Texas Christian University[1]

This idea that life on earth arose from a common single
cell amoeba and subsequently evolved into the huge
diversity of life we see around us was such a radical idea
that Darwin declined to publish it for twenty years. He
was very reluctant to include homo sapiens in his theory
of single cell amoeba origin and only vaguely suggested
this at the end of The Origin of Species. His wife was
a devout Christian and was deeply concerned regarding
the salvation of her dear husband's soul. Her pain may
have been the reason he delayed so long in publishing the
book.[2]

Darwin presented natural selection as a purposeless
dynamic, driven by chance and random variations within
species. Some variations were better suited for survival
and so were selected by nature. Others didn't cut the

mustard. Over vast amounts of time, these slight variations and adaptations could result in what Darwin called
'transmutation', the emergence of a new species; a natural
breeding process equivalent to the artificial breeding
process used by farmers occurred in nature.

It is worth focussing on Darwin's biggest problem in his
Theory of Evolution: the eye. When evolution sceptics
want to attack Darwin's theory, they point to the human
eye. How could something so complex have developed
through random mutation and natural selection, even
over millions of years?

In his sixth edition of *On the Origin of Species* (1872) Darwin states:

*...the difficulty of believing that a perfect and complex eye
could be formed by natural selection, though insuperable by
our imagination, should not be considered as subversive of the
theory.*

*How a nerve comes to be sensitive to light, hardly concerns us
more than how life itself originated; but I may remark that, as
some of the lowest organisms in which nerves cannot be detect-
ed, are capable of perceiving light, it does not seem impossible
that certain sensitive elements in their sarcode[3] should become
aggregated and develop into nerves, endowed with this special
sensitivity.[4]*

Through natural selection, different types of eyes have
emerged in evolutionary history – and the human eye is

not even the best one because blood vessels run across the surface of the retina instead of beneath it. It is easy for these vessels to proliferate or leak and impair vision.

If the eye were to have been made by God at the time of creation rather than developing by evolutionary principles then one has to say it was a botched design.

Having said that, I would hasten to add that (in my opinion) the theory of evolution in no way negates the hand of the 'Master of the Universe'. Every organism would seem to possess a self-perpetuating innate quality or genetic disposition which utilises spontaneous mutations for the benefit of the species. In my opinion, evolution is not an argument flaunted so regularly by Richard Dawkins as proof of his stand for atheism.

Furthermore, 'blind alleys' in evolution have been common occurrences. It has been estimated that during the evolutionary process early organisms made some forty unsuccessful attempts to develop a functioning eye. Primitive invertebrates were determined to see.

In brief, it would seem that the evolution of the eye has traced the following path: a simple light sensitive spot on the skin of some ancestral creature gave it some tiny survival advantage, perhaps allowing it to evade a predator; random changes then created a depression in the light sensitive patch, a deepening pit that made vision a little sharper. At the same time the pit's opening gradually narrowed, so light entered through a small aperture, like a pin-hole camera.

Every change had to confer a survival advantage no matter how slight. Eventually, the light-sensitive spot evolved into a retina, the layer of cells and pigment at the back of the eye. In time, a lens formed at the front of the eye and then the other elements that make up the human eye evolved. At some stage, colour vision evolved when the photoreceptor cells developed multiple pigments. In fact, eyes corresponding to every stage in this sequence have been found in existing living species.

The first animals with anything resembling an eye lived about 550 million years ago. Scientists have estimated that 364,000 years would be required for a camera-like eye to evolve from a light sensitive patch.

An Augustinian monk, Gregor Mendel, extended Darwin's hypothesis by tracking the inheritance traits in flower colour, leaf characteristics and seed shape, concluding that some traits are dominant, others recessive. When a dominant trait is crossed with a recessive trait, the dominant one wins out. But the recessive trait hangs around until it is mixed with another recessive trait and then it emerges.

Next followed August Weisman with the theory that in sexual reproduction the chromosomes join with each other, break down and recombine, resulting in all manner of combinations ensuring variety, a process known as genetic mutation. Nature selects the variations best suited to survival of the species, and the less effective combinations do not survive. The survival of the fittest – those with the biggest teeth, strongest muscles and the most testosterone – in the human species would result in male warriors.

Fifty years ago an English biologist, Francis Crick, won a Nobel Prize for co-discovering the structure of the DNA molecule whereby nature makes use of the evolutionary memory and wisdom of the universe stored in genes. At first this idea was expressed in relation to physical characteristics, but more recently this belief has been extended to include psychological and emotional traits as well.

Following Darwin's discoveries, it has become increasingly clear that human beings are latecomers on this planet and that we are seamlessly connected to and given life by all the life-forms that preceded us.[5] The human embryo starts as a single cell and, as it divides and redivides, it reproduces the history of all our primitive ancestors; the limbs develop, the cardiovascular system develops and then the immensely complicated neurological system evolves, all of this process tracing the path our primitive ancestors followed over the previous millions of years or more. Furthermore, the milieu that enabled life-forms to emerge may have taken fourteen billion years before that to emerge.

The post-Darwinian world recognises that there never was a perfect man or a perfect woman who fell into sin in an act of disobedience. That account is not true either historically or metaphorically. Human beings are emerging creatures; they are works in progress.[6]

As an example of our pre-human ancestry the vermiform

appendix is present in man, certain anthropoid apes, and the wombat. Morphologically, it is the undeveloped distal end of the large caecum, found in many lower mammals. Many herbivores are provided with a wide-lumened caecal diverticulum (outpouching) in which the bacteriolytic breakdown of cellulose takes place. The appendix in man is functionless and is the vestigial remnant of this organ found in earlier mammals. In man cellulose breakdown occurs in the acid-producing stomach. After a gastrectomy patients have to be warned against eating the pith of oranges – cellulose. The author had the experience of operating on a small bowel obstruction in a post gastrctomy patient. The cause? A large ball of undigested cellulose from orange pith.

How sad it is that the Christian faith has yet to make a concerted effort to accept this enchanted reality within its theological models and its liturgical life. Rather, many Christians choose to ignore the existence of Darwin and his discoveries, and there exists the implication that somehow the origin of species challenges accepted dogma and doctrine. How can theology be so blind as to deny that this too is part of some eternal plan? At least Darwin did not have to suffer the ignominy of a Roman Inquisition as did his ground-breaking predecessor Galileo!

In 2011, Pope Benedict XVI marked the holiest day of the year for Christians by stressing that humanity is not a random product of evolution. He emphasised the biblical account of creation in his Easter vigil homily, saying it was:

...wrong to think that at some point in some tiny corner of the cosmos there evolved randomly some species of living being capable of reasoning and of trying to find rationality within creation, or to bring rationality into it. If man were merely a random product of evolution in some place on the margins of the universe, then his life would make no sense or might even be a chance of nature. But no, reason is there at the beginning: creative, divine reason.[7]

In my humble opinion, the Pope fails to grasp that the two scenarios can be and have to be completely compatible. Evolution is with us, well and truly proven.

In the paradigm set out so far, we see strong evidence of a higher intelligence controlling cosmic and biological evolution. Controlling is an inappropriate term – rather should we say 'loosely directing', with potential for chance happenings along the journey. The evidence seems to be narrowing the 'differential diagnosis' as set out in the first part of this essay.

Difficulties are arising in accepting a designer God who is in absolute control of the universe. A God of supernatural theism does not seem to fit the bill. A God who intervenes in certain points of history, but is inexplicably restrained at other times, such as during the painful death of an innocent child, does not seem to fit our experience. A God who punishes unbelievers with eternal banishment, and rewards believers with eternal peace is hard to accept. According to this version of the Christian faith the only valid source is the Bible, considered to be inerrant and infallible. This sort of God does not seem to fit into an evolutionary universe and allow it to unfold with any kind of dignity. According to Bruce Sanguin, he would 'hog the agenda and dominate the whole affair'[8]. And where does he reside and hold court? Is it outside the cosmos? Surely if we are to home in on the real message of Jesus, then the 'Master of the Universe' is here in every object of His creation and not up in some mythical 'Heaven.'

'Heaven' is on earth, here and now. The intelligence we are seeing is one who is continually making room for His creatures to be free and to determine their own destiny.

'Cosmological' evolution is a new concept and American author and scholar Jim Gardner has compared it to the development of an embryo with its critical feedback mechanism. Interviewed by journalist Carter Phipps, a proponent of 'Evolutionary Spirituality', he states:

When an embryo begins to develop, every step in that development is not specified in advance by the DNA sequence. What happens is that the embryonic development reaches stage one, and then the tissue complex – that is, the embryo – starts sending signals back into the DNA, which modulates further expression of the gene into the new tissue. So it's a feedback loop, and the informational complexity inheres in that feedback process, not simply in the nucleotide sequence. That's truly the extraordinary miracle of it. The process of embryogenesis is exquisitely programmed to actually take account of the state of its own ongoing development and to use the suc-

ceeding stages of development as a sort of augmentation to the basic instruction manual, which the DNA contained in the genome.[9]

Carter Phipps then expands on his interview with Gardner:

Might humans, or intelligent life in whatever form, play that same role in the cosmological, universal evolutionary scheme of development? Might we in someway represent this feedback loop for the universe itself? Could our reflexion on the evolutionary process itself be an essential element not only in fulfilling the next stage of our own development but in creating the next novel stage of cosmogenesis?

...Gardner's hypothesis is an original and compelling evolutionary speculation! Creativity and novelty would seem to be written into the very cosmic narrative itself.[10]

Phipps believes mankind needs:

...a notion of God that is flexible enough to embrace the extraordinary development of knowledge of the past two centuries – a theological worldview, in other words, that could peer deeply into the natural world as revealed by science, and not flinch.[11]

Pertinent to where we find ourselves in this narrative, we're led to Alfred Whitehead, a contemporary of Scottish philosopher and mathematician Bertrand Russell, who began a line of philosophical thought in the twenti-

eth century (1929) called 'process philosophy', later taken
up by academic Charles Hartshorne at his posts at Harvard, the University of Chicago, and the University of
Texas, where he applied process philosophy to theology.

Phipps explains:

*Hartshorne rejected the ancient vision of omnipotence so com-
mon in the traditional understanding of God. He put forth a
god who is actually developing as the universe itself moves forward in time. In this sense, process theology would suggest that
we all participate to some degree in the being and becoming of
God, in the very evolution of divinity. We are part of God's
self, so to speak, and as we participate in the development of
this universe, so too do we, in some fundamental way, participate in God's self-development. Paradoxically, by placing
limits on God's perfection, Hartshorne and Whitehead simultaneously expanded the depth of his or her being. They opened
the door to seeing God not simply as an object of distant worship but as an intimate subject in whose ongoing creative self-
development we can each participate.*

*... By drawing powerful connections between the evolutionary
dynamics of the universe and the very being of the divine they
helped set the stage for a new evolutionary theology to emerge
in our time, one whose picture of divinity was at least congru-
ent with a scientifically revealed universe ... if people in this
day and age are going to believe in a God, then they need a
God that is believable.* [12]

Another thought along these same lines is offered by Brian Swimme:

The earth wants to come into a deeper way of reflecting on itself. The invention of the eye is an example. It's almost like the life process wants to deepen its awareness. It first invented eyes that were made out of calcite, a mineral. It was so desperate to see, it actually found a way using a mineral. Scientists estimate that life invented eyesight forty separate times. It wasn't an accident. It is as if the whole system of life was going to find a way to see one way or another. So what's the essence of life? Life wants a richer experience. Life wants to see. And we come out of this same process. We also want to see, we want to know, we want to understand deeply. That is a further development of this basic impulse in life itself.[13]

Is process theology too much of a quantum leap to digest in our search for a differential diagnosis? Certainly it has attractive elements and seems to fit into the era in which we find ourselves. It brings God closer to our very being, more believable – working alongside us as a brother and participating in our day to day existence rather than a remote object of omnipotence. It steers well clear of the supernatural. It would seem to have no conflict with Jesus's original teaching as distinct from the superimposed recordings and reported supernatural events inserted later by the writers of the gospels.

NOTES

1. Darren J. N. Middleton, *When faith meets religion,* Polebridge Press, Salem, 2008, p. 131

2. Discussed by Bruce Sanguin, *Darwin, divinity, and the dance of the cosmos,* Wood Lake Publishing, Kelowna, 2007, pp. 101-125.

3. Sarcode refers to protoplasm, the living contents of a cell.

4. Charles Darwin, *The Origin of species,* 1859, p. 191. Online at http://www.talkorigins.org/faqs/origin/chapter6.html, accessed 16 April 2013.

5. Bruce Sanguin, op. cit., pp. 103-104.

6. John Shelby Spong, *A New Christianity for a new world,* Harper Collins, San Francisco, 2001, pp. 123-124.

7. Pope Benedict XVI, *Easter address 2011.* Online at http://www.vatican.va/holy_father/benedict_xvi/messages/urbi/documents/hf_ben-xvi_mes_20110424_urbi-easter_en.html, accessed 16 April 2013.

8. Bruce Sanguin, op. cit., p. 121.

9. Carter Phipps, *A New dawn for cosmology: an interview with James Gardner,* Enlighten Next magazine, Issue 19 Spring-Summer 2001.

Online at http://www.enlightennext.org/ magazine/j33/gardner.asp.

10. Carter Phipps, *Evolutionaries: unlocking the spiritual and cultural potential of science's greatest idea*, Harper Perennial, New York, 2012, pp. 123-124.

11. ibid., p. 355.

12. ibid., p. 344.

13. Brian Swimme in Phipps, p. 318.

7

On Theism and Deism

Religious and theological integrity is possible as and when discourse about God declines the attempt to take God's point of view.
Rowan Williams

Archbishop of Canterbury[1]

We have described theism as it developed through various civilisations. Theism conceives of God as personal, present and active in the governance and organisation of the world and the universe. Theism describes the classical conception of God that is found in Christianity, Judaism, Islam and some forms of Hinduism. The use of the word theism began during the scientific revolution of the seventeenth century in order to distinguish it from deism which contended that God, though transcendent and supreme, did not intervene in the natural world and could be known rationally but not through revelation.

The distinction between these terms seems to have fallen into disfavour as the author, on questioning a number of clergy, inclucluding a lecturer in a theological college, found them all puzzled by the distinction between the two terms.

The author's own interest in the distinction was aroused by Robert Nairn[2] in his treatise on Masonic practices and beliefs.

Christian deism is a standpoint that believes in the moral teachings – but not divinity – of Jesus. Christian deists see no paradox in adopting the values and ideals espoused by Jesus without believing he was God. Deists reject atheism. Deism holds that God does not intervene with the functioning of the natural world in any way, allowing it to run according to the laws of nature that he configured when he created all things. God is conceived to be wholly transcendent and never immanent. In other words God is conceived to exist apart from the material universe and not permanently invading the universe.[3]

For deists, human beings can only know God via reason and the observation of nature but not by revelation or supernatural manifestations (such as miracles) – phenomena which deists regard with caution if not scepticism.

Christian deists believe that Jesus Christ was a deist. Jesus taught that there are two basic laws of God governing humankind. The first law is that life comes from God and we are to use it as God intends, as illustrated in Jesus' parable of the talents. The second law is that God intends for human beings to live by love for each other, as illustrated in Jesus' parable of the good Samaritan.

Deists are opposed to religious orthodoxy, dogma and doctrine, all of which they argue lead inevitably to corruption and intolerance. Deism acknowledges that most religions contain within them a basic core of rational truth and understanding of God. Nevertheless, all have fallen away due to the corrupting influence of supernatural religious beliefs and superstitions. In the evidence-based reasoning we're attempting to follow in order to arrive at a 'diagnosis', deism has many attractive elements that seem to have fallen by the wayside over the last century.

NOTES

1. Rowan Williams, *On Christian theology: challenges in contemporary theology,* Wiley, 2000, p. xii.

2. Robert Nairn is an Australian Capital Territory-based member of the Australia and New Zealand Masonic Research Council.

3. The author, whilst being sympathetic to much of the deists' beliefs, would disagree with this aspect – at least in 2012! Refer to Chapter 14: *The Spirit behind the universe,* p. 101.

8

Atheism

To believe in God is childish
To deny the existence of God is madness
To search for God is the answer.

Felix Dahn

Ein Kampf un Rom[1]

Atheism is a difficult term to define. In the previous section, a distinction was made between theism and deism.
Deists may reasonably be termed anti-theists but not
atheists. Atheists, in common parlance, are those who
reject any belief in God and more particularly a belief in
the personal God believed in by members of the Abra-
hamic religions – Christianity, Judaism, and Islam.
Avowed atheists dismiss supernatural entities of any
kind.

Atheists mount their arguments for disbelief along the
following lines. The problem of evil is perhaps the atheists' biggest weapon in their challenge to theism. Scottish
philosopher David Hume (1711-1776) echoing the Greek
philosopher Epicurus:

*Is God willing to prevent evil, but not able? If so, he is impo-
tent. Is he able, but not willing? Then he is malevolent. Is he
both able and willing? Whence then is evil? Is he neither able
nor willing? Then why call him God?*[2]

Augustine's argument against this is that evil is unfortu-
nate but unavoidable because of mans' free will.[3]

Atheists will argue that we do not believe in things until
evidence is provided for them, and that God is no excep-
tion.

The cosmological argument that the universe must have
a cause, namely God, was refuted by Scottish philosopher
and mathematician Bertrand Russell (1872-1970) when
he stated that the world was a mere brute fact which
stood in need of no further explanation.[4]

The presence of highly complex objects in the world such
as living organisms is a more difficult question for the
atheists to explain in the absence of a supernatural being.

The question of miracles is not confined to atheists and
will be dealt with in a later section of this essay.

Religious belief has traditionally provided human beings
with a reason to think that their individual lives have a
purpose. Atheism, on the other hand, has generally taught
that individual human beings and humanity as a whole
have no purpose in the universe, and that they will be

annihilated in the course of time when the earth finally becomes uninhabitable.

It seems to me that atheists have adopted a position which is very hard to justify on the evidence available and is predominantly based on what they can't believe rather than what they do believe. Anti-theism, the inability to believe in theism, is understandable. Theism is defined in the Oxford dictionary as 'belief in the existence of a God supernaturally revealed to man as creator and supreme ruler of the universe'. Theism, it seems to me, has been developed as a human coping measure; designed to give security and reassurance, to say nothing of the power that resided in those who were self-appointed in the dispensation of 'eternal life.' Atheists have difficulty with the doctrines and dogmas so long clasped to the bosoms of the orthodox religions. So do I, but I do not put myself in the category of an atheist. Anti-theist perhaps, but not atheist.

The orthodox religions have not sought to move on from the 17th century concept of a God up there in the sky removed from the cosmos, sitting in heaven listening to the throngs of the faithful singing His praises and dispensing justice as He sees fit or withholding it at His whim. That definition may have served a purpose in giving security to the multitudes over the centuries, but the need is for the church to move on into the twenty-first century and get the right 'diagnosis' which fits all the developing evidence accumulated by modern scholars who come from all persuasions – Catholic, Protestant, Jewish – and are more or less united in their views. We are, or should be, all dedicated to truth and integrity, whatever the cost.

It seems to me that the atheist's leap of faith is far greater than that of any orthodox believer. We are now referring to those who specifically believe everything created came into being purely by chance rather than the anti-theists from whom a distinction must be made, i.e. those who simply reject orthodox Christian doctrines.

What about agnostics (a-gnostic = not known)? I think most agnostics are lazy, shrug their shoulders, are indifferent, and permeate themselves with the drab mental furniture of the spiritually uninspired.

We can follow life through from the Big Bang to the single cell amoebae as the first forms of life, to the dinosaurs, and on to the higher forms of life, culminating in the enormous complexity of *homo sapiens*. The very complexities of the physiology of the human body are understood on a very primitive level using explanations and language that are plausible and seem to work, but the mechanisms on a micro level have yet to be unravelled. And all this developed due to chance? And it all functions and is by and large self-sufficient except for the occasional call on a repair man who may or may not be able to help?

In simple physics, objects fall at thirty-two feet per second squared and continue to do so without human intervention, and Halley's Comet turns up every seventy-six years without our help. All this makes Man look very insignificant and has caused him from time immemorial to search for an outside source. His searches have by and large followed the same pattern from the early Egyptians up to the present day.

Stephen Hawking has an interesting contribution to make in this regard:

Science seems to have uncovered a set of laws that, within the limits set by the uncertainty principle, tell us how the universe will develop with time, if we know its state at any one time. These laws may have originally been decreed by God, but it appears that he has since left the universe to evolve according to them and does not now intervene in it. But how did he choose the initial state or configuration of the universe? What were the 'boundary conditions' at the beginning of time?

One possible answer is to say that God chose the initial configuration of the universe for reasons that we cannot hope to understand. This would certainly have been within the power of an omnipotent being, but if he had started it off in such an incomprehensible way, why did he choose to let it evolve according to laws that we could understand? The whole history of science has been the gradual realisation that events do not happen in an arbitrary manner, but that they reflect a certain underlying order, which may or may not be divinely inspired.[5]

And again, a little further on, Stephen Hawking makes a profound and pertinent observation:

The laws of science, as we know them at present, contain many fundamental numbers, like the size of the electric charge of the

electron and the ratio of the masses of the proton and the elec-
tron. We cannot, at the moment at least, predict the values of
these numbers from theory – we have to find them by obser-
vation. It may be that one day we shall discover a complete
unified theory that predicts them all. ... The remarkable fact is
that the values of these numbers seem to have been very finely
adjusted to make possible the development of life. For exam-
ple if the electric charge of the electron had been only slightly
different, stars either would have been unable to burn hydro-
gen and helium, or else they would not have exploded. ... It
seems clear that there are relatively few ranges of values for
the numbers that would allow the development of any form of
intelligent life. Most sets of values would give rise to universes
that, although they might be very beautiful, would contain no
one able to wonder at that beauty. One can take this either as
evidence of a divine purpose in Creation and the choice of the
laws of science or as support for the strong anthropic[6] princi-
ple.[7]

...Even if there is only one possible unified theory, it is just a
set of rules and equations. What is it that breathes fire into the
equations and makes a universe for them to describe? The usu-
al approach of science of constructing a mathematical model
cannot answer the question of why there should be a universe
for the model to describe. Why does the universe go to all the
bother of existing? Is the unified theory so compelling that it
brings about its own existence? Or does it need a creator, and,
if so, does he have any other effect on the universe? And who
created him?[8]

This section on atheism would be incomplete without reference to today's greatest protagonist for their cause, Richard Dawkins. His best seller, *The God Delusion*[9] makes interesting reading.

This book is predominantly aimed against the theist or supernatural aspects of Christianity and as such is quite logical and promotes no argument. It is heavily anecdotal, at times trite, and trivialises the debate, invoking heavy sarcasm. Dawkins is cynical and overplays the invective giving the impression at times that he is trying to convince himself. He spends many pages rebutting that which modern Christian scholars accept are clearly errors or inventions in biblical writings.

Dawkins constantly invokes Darwin to support his argument and seems to assume that evolution, *ipso facto*, is sufficient to rule out the necessity for a higher spiritual being in cosmos creation. The book has no positive answers to offer as it is totally devoted to debunking, being full of hyperbolic rhetoric. Thankfully he treats the writings of Einstein with due respect and Einstein's important contributions to these matters will be mentioned in later segments.

In summary then, the diagnosing physician, on the clinical evidence presented, regrettably, has to again follow his gut feeling and reject the atheists' hypothesis that everything came from nothing. His gut feeling admittedly is influenced by the horrible barrenness and emptiness that follows from a belief in atheism but is swayed also by the viewpoint that the complexity and orderliness of the cosmos and life in all its forms could not possibly have arisen by chance, or even by evolution alone, as Dawkins would have us believe.

NOTES

1. Felix Dahn, *Ein Kampt um Rom*, Breitopf & Sartel, Leipzig, 1876 (3 vols) p. 1296.

2. David Hume, *Enquiries concerning human understanding,* Ed. L. A. Selby-Bigge, 3rd ed. revised P. H. Nidditch, Clarendon Press, Oxford, 1975.

3. Augustine, *De Libero Arbitrio*, trans. Dom Mark Pontifex, Newman Press, London, 1955.

4. Espoused in a 1948 BBC radio debate between Bertrand Russell and Jesuit priest and philosopher historian Father Frederick Copleston at http://www.philvaz.com/apologetics/p20.htm.

5. Stephen Hawking, *A Brief history of time,* Bantam Press, London, 1988, p. 129.

6. Astronomer Brandon Carter's anthropic principle, expounded in 1974, hypothesized that what scientists had referred to as 'anthropic coincidences' – the circumstances that allow mankind to exist - are part of the universe's very structure and that chance has nothing to do with it. In simple terms, we exist because the universe is the way it is.

7. Stephen Hawking, op. cit., pp. 131-132.

8. ibid., p. 184.

9. Richard Dawkins, *The God delusion,* Bantam
Books, London, 2006.

9

Searches in Theism

Homo sapiens' arrival in the universe is a relatively recent event in the big scheme of things. The Darwinian skills for the survival of the fittest and smartest of the species found him honing his hunting skills and refining his combating skills against his opposing tribesmen so that his own individual survival could be assured. As man became more civilised, these instincts have been required to be suppressed, and in the institutionalised church became referred to as 'sins' and the 'working of the Devil', i.e. an outside force and therefore not a result of man's own actions (refer Adam and Eve story in Genesis).

Somewhere along this line of evolution, as the brain of *homo sapiens* developed and he outstripped all his four-legged rivals, he became self-aware or self-conscious. This was an enormous advance and immediately differentiated man from all other creatures, which lived for the day with no thought of where they came from or where they were going and that death was inevitable.

Self-awareness led to anxiety and a deep need for secu-

rity, so man invented theism, initially multi-theism and
finally monotheism.

The Ancient Egyptians[1]

The Ancient Egyptians had a sophisticated system 5000
years ago. Formal religious practice centred on the
pharaoh, the king of Egypt. Although he was a human, the
pharaoh was believed to be descended from the gods, and
upon his death he became fully deified. In life he acted as
the intermediary between his people and the gods. On a
divergent note, one cannot help but be struck by the sim-
ilarity of this concept to that introduced in John's Gospel,
'the Word made flesh,' where St John contended that Jesus
was with God from the beginning. One can follow the
development of this concept in Christianity through the
decades of the first century. St Paul, writing around 60
CE, was of the view that Jesus' deification came at the
time of 'his resurrection from the dead' (Romans 1:4). St
Mark's Gospel, written a decade or more later, declares
Jesus' deification at the time of his baptism in the Jordan
River. Moving on to the eighties CE, when Matthew and
Luke were written, the birth tradition was introduced,
with Jesus' deification occuring a step earlier, at the time
of His conception. John's Gospel was written five to fif-
teen years after Matthew and Luke, at around 95 CE, and
here we find the deification moves back yet another step
and is in line with the pharaoh tradition. Not that deification was restricted in those days. Anyone who was anyone claimed connection with a deity. Alexander the Great
was claimed not to have a mortal father and Julius Caesar
had the goddess Venus as his mother.

The practices of Egyptian religion were centred around efforts to provide for the gods and gain their favour. Another important aspect of the religion was the belief in the afterlife and funerary practices. The Egyptians made great efforts to ensure the survival of their souls after death, providing tombs, grave goods and offerings to preserve the bodies and spirits of the deceased.

At various periods during their 3,000-year span, the ancient Egyptians moved towards monotheism, although never completely. The sun god Ra occupied a very prominent place at one stage, appearing on cue every morning and disappearing in the evening.

In line with early Christianity, the Ancient Egyptians believed their gods were domiciled in the sky, hence the architecture of the pyramids. The shape of the pyramid represents the shafts of sunlight one sees protruding through breaks in the clouds, and each pyramid is a pharaoh's attempt to reach up to his god.[2]

During the late Old Kingdom and the First Intermediate Period, the Egyptians gradually came to believe that each person, not only the pharaoh, had spiritual characteristics unique to each individual, and that after undergoing a final judgement known as the 'Weighing of the Heart' the possibility of a paradisiacal afterlife extended to everyone.

The Egyptians produced numerous prayers and hymns, written in the form of poetry. Hymns were written to praise particular deities and were written on papyri and on temple walls, and were probably recited as part of the rituals. In the New Kingdom, the prayers asked for blessings, help of forgiveness for wrongdoing, and were part of a movement towards a more personal interaction with a deity, formerly not believed possible.

A final word. Though the priesthood had started out simply, with relatively few temples, in the later dynasties the temples expanded into the hundreds. With such a growth, a large bureaucracy was needed to keep the temples in good standing: and thus the small priesthood of the earlier Egyptians grew from an estimated hundred priests into the thousands, and with it came a priestly hierarchy! It ever was thus!

Greek Philosophy

Greek Philosophy put its major emphasis on the human intellect[3]. Plato explained that there was, beyond the world of perceivable objects, another world, the world of 'Forms.' Everyday things change and are corruptible, but the 'Forms' are perfect, unchanging and eternal. They are reality. The greatest human accomplishment is to know the 'Forms' in themselves, and to do this, humans must turn inwards, away from the distraction of things and other people. They do this by means of their intellect. The soul or intellect is non-material; it can exist separated from the body and in fact did exist prior to being united with its present body. It is the soul, not the body, which attains knowledge of the 'Forms.' The body is a passing thing; it corrupts and dies. The soul lives on. We can see what a huge influence Greek thought had on the early Christian church.

To digress for a moment; this thought parallels Bhuddhist and Hindu teaching – belief in rebirth. The present Dalai Lama is his predecessor, reborn. Buddhist doctrine holds that there are 'five aggregates', according to which, what we call a human being is a complex of five elements – feeling (pleasure, pain and indifference), perception, mental formations (our dispositions, our character), and consciousness. The person is not to be identified with any of the above. In other words, the me is not my feelings, not my perceptions, not my dispositions, not my character, not my consciousness. The me is not these elements themselves but, rather, the me is what holds these elements or 'aggregates'. But if the me is not the five 'aggregates' what is there to be reborn, what is it that migrates from one body to the next? How do Buddhists reconcile these two doctrines? Buddhists are fully aware of this problem and address it but their arguments are beyond the scope of this brief essay.[4]

These are interesting concepts from Buddhism and probably should be carried into Christian thought, although I have not come across it in any reading. The me as it moves to the Christian heaven would be divorced from its genetic makeup, its Irish predisposition to behave badly at times (I refer to my own genes), or even those commendable genes that make some people more charitable than others. But then environmental factors come into the equation and so the philosophical thought meanders on ...

Aristotle developed Plato's ideas on the 'Forms' still further. Aristotle lessened the dualism of body and soul in the human being. However it was Platonic Greek thought that mostly influenced the early Christians. Early Christianity saw the visible world of phenomena, whatever can be sensed, as an exterior reflection of a more perfect world, and a very imperfect imitation of that world. The Christians were exhorted to look beyond the visible signs in space and time to that reality to which the signs referred. The Hebrew world view expressed through a Platonic Greek way of thinking was the underpinning of Christian thought. This system would serve the European mind very well for many centuries.

The towering figure in Greek philosophy was Socrates (469-399 BCE). He was charismatic with a somewhat eccentric lifestyle and spent all his time in unpaid discussion with whomsoever would join him. Among them was Plato who dedicated his career and writings to the philosophy of Socrates, in the process of which he immortalised both of them. In Plato's *The Apology of Socrates* Plato sets out Socrates speeches made in defence at his trial at which he was sentenced to death. Many perennial philosophical debates are raised by Socrates including the relationship between morals and religion. Is morality possible without belief in god?[5]

Another useful suggestion of Socrates was acquiring some understanding of why we do things. This is often a prerequisite to change and is especially true when talking about repetitive patterns of behaviour that do not serve us well. This is what Socrates meant when he said,

'The unexamined life is not worth living.' That more of us do not take his advice is testimony to the hard work and potential embarrassment such self-examination demands.

Before leaving Greek philosophy, passing mention should be made of Epicurus (341-271 BCE). For him and his followers, the one and only thing valuable in itself was pleasure. But by no means did he recommend a continuous round of orgies and banquets. His meaning of pleasure was absence of pain, both physical and mental.[6] Whereas Epicurus' focus was on the individual, Buddhism follows a similar line in the personal attainment of 'nirvana'. In Buddhist Bhutan the king goes to great lengths to measure the level of 'National Happiness'; far more important in his eyes than the national economy! A commendable philosophy – let everyone be free from pain and anxiety. Helping those around you to do so will probably help you to achieve it too – and if so, help them.

In his book *Too Soon Old, Too Late Smart*, United States psychiatrist Dr Gordon Livingstone states: 'The three components of happiness are something to do, someone to love, and something to look forward to.' Furthermore, 'only by embracing our mortality can we be happy in the time we have'.[7]

Religion in Ancient Rome

Religion in Ancient Rome encompassed the religious beliefs and cult practices regarded by the Romans as indigenous and central to their identity as a people. Romans thus offered homage to innumerable deities who influenced every aspect of both the natural world and human affairs. The establishment of these deities was credited to Rome's divine ancestors and founders.

Participation in traditional religious rituals was considered a practical and moral necessity in personal, domestic and public life. Romans could offer homage to any deity or any combination of deities as long as it did not offend the 'custom of ancestors,' that is, Roman tradition. Good relations between mortals and the divine were maintained by piety, which meant the correct offering of ritual and divine honours, especially in the form of sacrifice. In return, the gods were likely to benefit their worshippers. Impieties could provoke divine wrath against the State. Some Romans claimed divine ancestry to justify their position among the ruling class, most notably Julius Caesar, who asserted that he had descended from the goddess Venus. Even the most sceptical among Rome's intellectual elite, such as Cicero, acknowledged the necessity of religion as a form of social order despite its obvious irrational elements.

As Rome extended its influence and presence throughout the Mediterranean world, it encountered and absorbed foreign deities and practices. Some were officially embraced, others tolerated and a few condemned as alien hysteria, magic or superstition. Christianity was superstition, or atheism, or both; druidism was thought to employ human sacrifice; Judaism was merely tolerated.

The era of Christian hegemony began with the conversion of Constantine I. In 391, Christianity became the state religion to the exclusion of all other cults, which were condemned collectively as 'pagan.' However, many pre-Christian beliefs and practices survived in Christian festivals and traditions.

The Emperor Constantine (who championed Christianity but never officially joined) was confident that a common faith across his territory could contribute to the unity he sought. So he called together church leaders, being careful to secure a majority for the position he espoused, and strongly encouraged them to develop a statement of faith that would define Christianity for all his citizens.

The bishops began this process by meeting in Nicaea in 325 CE. The baggage the bishops brought contained more than clothing. It included both theological and political agendas. Western and eastern sides of the empire used the session, and many that followed it, to exacerbate their already raging conflict. Church councils and military battles fed on each other for at least forty years. Murder, betrayal and royal intrigue were part of the complicated, messy undertaking.

Finally, after extensive bloodshed and manoeuvring, a creed was produced, the Nicene Creed. That creed defined the faith and thereby branded the heretics. Those guilty of the newly defined heresies were, of course, immediately banished from the church.

...To those giving leadership to the church in the fourth century, the greatest evil on the horizon was a misunderstanding of the relationship of Jesus to God. They settled that concern on the side of high Christology: Jesus and God were the same essence.

Other issues were left untouched. The Nicene Creed has been called the creed with the hole in the middle. It states how Jesus was born, and describes how and why he died. No mention is given of his teachings or acts of compassion, even though they take up the majority of the pages of the biblical accounts.

...The Nicene Creed was designed to meet the particular issues of the time and place of its birth ...Sadly, it has also tended to freeze the faith into a form best suited to the setting in which it was composed.[8]

Like Roman Emperors before him, Constantine was also hailed as divine, Son of God, and Lord. But he was not, as in the creed 'begotten and not made' or 'of one substance' and 'one being' with God which was Bishop Athanasius's position in the debate. This of course put Jesus above the status of the Emperor, and within a few years Constantine realised this, and adopted Bishop Arius's position, who had been an advocate of a lesser status for Jesus, below that of God. His imperial successors pursued this for much of the fourth century but without success.[9]

The church moved far from its roots when it argued at Nicaea over whether Jesus was of a similar essence, or the same essence, as God. It was not a huge further step when the First Council of Constantinople in 381 CE declared the doctrine of the Trinity and stamped out any further debate. This step, by its threefold nature, completely separates Christianity from Judaism and Islam and even Hinduism, all of which accept the twofold nature of God.

Disputes continued, of course, and in the eleventh century there was a Great Schism. The issue was whether the Holy Spirit 'proceeds' from 'the Father' or from 'the Father and the Son'. The Western church affirmed the latter, and the Eastern church the former. In 1054 CE Christianity split in two over the issue, producing Roman Catholicism and Eastern Orthodoxy. Each side excommunicated the other![10]

What political power and vested interests we see in committee decisions when they set out doctrines that are laid down as being established by God! Jesus himself, I am sure, would not have been able to think His way through the logic of the Trinity!

Interestingly, Sir Isaac Newton, around 1660, was persuaded that 'the revealed documents gave no support to the Trinitarian doctrines which were due to late falsifications.'[11] Shortly after, at the age of twenty-two, Newton invented the differential calculus.

Jesus himself refused to give clear answers when asked about his role. He never requested 'worship me.' His challenge was 'Follow me.' I firmly believe that those passages in the gospels, 'He that has seen me has seen the Father,' and again 'No man cometh to the Father but by me,' are editorial insertions by the gospel writers and reflect the evolving deification of Jesus in the developing church at the time they were written some forty to fifty years after Jesus' death (75-85 CE). Paul, writing much earlier in the sixth decade, put Jesus deification at the time of his death. He had no doubt Jesus was 'born of a woman' and was fully human during His life.

NOTES

1. http://en.wikipedia.org/wiki/ Ancient_Egyptian_religion. Accessed 31 January 2011.

2. Concept espoused by Egyptian guide Hassan during tour of the great pyramids, 2004.

3. Robert Crotty, *The Jesus question: the historical search,* Harper Collins, London, 1996, pp. 9-10.

4. Edward Craig, *Philosophy: A Very short introduction,* Oxford University Press, London, 2002, pp. 35-43.

5. Plato, *The Last days of Socrates*, trans. Hugh Tredennick, Penguin Books, London, 2003.

6. Diogenes Laertius, *Lives of the eminent philosophers,* Harvard University Press, Boston, 1972.

7. Gordon Livingstone, *Too soon old, too late smart,* Da Capo Press, Cambridge, 2004.

8. Jack Good, *The Dishonest Church,* Rising Star
Press, Bend, 2003, pp. 78-79.
9. Marcus Borg, *Speaking Christian,* Harper
One, San Francisco, 2001, p. 217.
10. ibid., p. 214.
11. Carl Sagan, *Cosmos,* MacDonald Futura
Publishers, London, 1980, p. 68.

10

The History of Judaism

The history of Judaism is long and complex and a brief synopsis only is set out here.

The formation of ancient Israel is recorded in the Torah or Pentateuch, the first five books of the Bible. The intention of the sacred books of the Torah was never to provide an accurate history of ancient Israel. They were written to give the people of Israel their way of life and their essential teaching and direction. It does reflect a historical epoch but the recorded detail is largely mythological.

The Hebrew Scriptures describe three major phases in the history of the children of Israel. The first was the patriarchal era, the time of the founding fathers or patriarchs (Abraham, Isaac and Jacob). The second phase was the Exodus when they escaped from Egypt, and the final phase was their conquest of the land of Canaan and their settlement in it.[1]

However, 'according to archaeologists working in Israel, there is no archaeological evidence that any of the patriarchs – Abraham, Noah, Moses or Joshua – ever existed:

there was no exile of the Jews in Egypt, no heroic Exodus and no violent conquest of Canaan.'[2] Even the historical existence of David and Solomon and that golden epoch of Jewish history beginning in the twelfth century BC, when the vast cities of Megiddo, Hazor and Jezreel were built, presents an archaeological problem.[3] The most likely scenario would seem to be that the Jews did not arrive from outside Canaan and subdue the indigenous people but were just another local tribe (among many others) that separated out, having developed their own gods (plural).[4]

The above supports the view that the Bible was first assembled by Jews returning from the 'second exile,' that is the Babylonian exile, which is well documented, as distinct from the so-called 'first' Egyptian exile, which is of doubtful historical veracity. In order to justify these claims to the land, the Covenant with God was invented. No-one, however, questions the fact that monotheism was a uniquely Israelite creation within the Middle East.

The Israelites were taken into captivity in 586 BCE by the Babylonians under Nebuchadnezzer. In 539, however, Babylon was captured by Cyrus, a Persian king who had also defeated the Medes and the Lydians. He and his followers spread Zoroastrianism throughout the Middle East. Cyrus freed the Jews and allowed them back to their homeland. It is no accident that Judaism, and therefore Christianity and Islam, share many features of Zoroastrianism, which goes back earlier than 1,000 BCE. Life after death, resurrection, judgement, heaven and paradise were all Zoroastrian ideas first, as were hell and the devil.[5]

Robert Crotty, an ordained passionist priest and archaeologist has made an informed and scholarly contribution to the debate on the beginnings of Judaism in his book *Three Revolutions*. His conclusion is that there is very little and probably no historical basis for the writings of the Old Testament:

Among nomadic, non-agricultural people such as the ancient Hebrews, theism evolved into a form of tribal monotheism. All theistic power was vested in a single deity, who tended to be exclusively male. He was seen as a mighty warrior who led wandering people into battle and a great protector watching over the lands they inhabited ...Such tribal activities as the corporate efforts to please this deity, to obey this deity, and to worship this deity were considered necessary to the survival of the tribe itself. Tribal monotheistic gods were depicted as jealous of their prerogatives, angry when offended, punitive when disobeyed, and beneficent when pleased.

But limits were clearly placed on the power of these deities, for their authority and their dictates appeared to stop at the edges of the tribe's boundaries. The Egyptian god ruled Egypt, the Assyrian god ruled Assyria and the Philistine god ruled the land of the Philistines...At this time a universal god could not yet be imagined.[6]

Later, universal monotheism took hold, but it took different cultural and liturgical forms. Christianity became its western form; Islam its Middle Eastern form; Hinduism, Buddhism and Confucianism its Far Eastern form; Judaism was scattered throughout all of the above.

The next inevitable step was taken by the hierarchy to reassure their flock: our deity is the only true deity, the truth of this deity has been given only to us and it was given by direct revelation, so its truth cannot be questioned. Since we are the sole designated recipients of this revelation, we alone can interpret it properly, and our interpretation cannot be challenged.

Thus the flocks of all cultures were reassured and their security maintained.

Unfortunately, all the theocracies have made God in the image of man, whereas the uncomfortable evidence would seem to indicate otherwise – man is an incidental by-product in His big scheme of things.

The other big drawback of theism is that it denies that the world, including us, shares in God's being. That would not be the experience of most people, and here I would add that spiritualty is by no means confined to the religious; far from it. Experiences of spirituality are to be found in many areas: in most artistic creations, in music frequently, in nature, in meditation – the list goes on and on.

In defence of Judaism, one has to admit that Jews are always more comfortable than Christianity when it comes to an open tradition and more comfortable questioning the ways of 'the Master of the Universe' and why some things happen as they do. Poor Tevye in *Fiddler on the Roof* has no hesitation in declaring to the Almighty, 'Would it have upset some vast eternal plan if I had been born a rich man?' The traditional Jewish capacity to engage in dialectic thinking is refreshing and stimulating, but it seems not to be welcomed in Christian circles.

NOTES

1. Robert Crotty, *The Jesus question: the historical search,* Harper Collins, London, 1996, pp. 72.

2. Peter Watson, *Ideas: A History from fire to Freud,* Phoenix Paperback, London, 2006, p. 206.

3. ibid., p. 207.

4. Tel Aviv Professor of Archeology Israel Finkelstein in an interview with Peter Watson, in *Ideas,* Ch. 7.

5. Peter Watson, op. cit., pp. 152-5

6. John Shelby Spong, *A New Christianity for a new world,* Harper Collins, London, 2001, pp. 47-48.

11

The Quest for the Historical Jesus

What a useless quest! The historical Jesus can add nothing to the Christ of Faith, I hear you say. Who cares what the historical Jesus was like? I have my faith regardless of what you turn up, and anyway we know enough about Him from the synoptic Gospels to make any search irrelevant and *unreliable*.

And so the argument goes on.

But what if, just what if, his whole life and teaching has been hijacked and manipulated by the early Church, with this one and that one adding or subtracting to what he said according to their understanding of what He was on about. And what did the First Council at Nicaea in 325 CE think Jesus was on about, and did they agree or did they have to vote on it as a committee? Not important you say! Well, I happen to think that it is particularly important, especially for our integrity.

There have been three eras of quests for the historical Jesus, the most recent commencing in the 1980s and stimulated by recent archaeological finds, knowledge about social structures of the times and changes in methodologies as practised by members of the Jesus Seminar at the Westar Institute.[1]

The first quest started in the seventeenth century and ended around 1906 when Albert Schweitzer published *The Quest for the Historical Jesus*. This book had enormous impact, coming as it did from a man who was a PhD in both organ music and theology. He terminated his career as an organ recitalist to study medicine at the age of thirty-one and then built a hospital in Lambarene, French Gabon, Africa, where he spent the rest of his days as a medical missionary. One has to listen to someone prepared to act on his convictions. His conclusions, however, I believe have been largely superseded by the modern methodology of twenty-first century Christian scholars.

What definite historical facts can we establish about the historical Jesus and are there historical references to Jesus outside the Bible?

Flavius Josephus[2] (c. 37-100 CE) was born to an aristocratic Jewish family, served as a priest and later became the commander of Jewish forces in Galilee following the revolt against Rome that began in 66 CE. He surrendered to the Roman forces in July 67 CE commanded by Flavius Vespasian and his son Titus, both of whom subsequently became roman emperors. Remarkably, his life was spared and he was freed and he became a Roman adviser and observer at the siege of Jerusalem and destruction of the Temple in 70 CE. He was granted Roman citizenship and went to live in Rome under Flavian patronage (hence his first name), where he wrote all his known historical works.

In *Jewish Antiquities* Book 18, Chapter 3, paragraph 3 Josephus writes:

Now there was about this time Jesus, a wise man, if it be lawful to call him a man: for he was a doer of wonderful works, a teacher of such men as receive the truth with pleasure. He drew over to him both many of the Jews and many of the Gentiles. He was [the] Christ. And when Pilate, at the suggestion of the principal men among us, had condemned him to the cross, those that loved him at the first did not forsake him; for he appeared to them alive again the third day, as the divine prophets had foretold these and ten thousand other wonderful things concerning him. And the tribe of Christians, so named for him, are not extinct to this day.[3]

In *Jewish Antiquities* Book 18, Chapter 5, paragraph 2 Josephus writes:

Now some of the Jews thought that the destruction of Herod's army came from God, and that very justly, as a punishment of what he did against John, that was called the Baptist: for Herod slew him, who was a good man, and commanded the Jews to exercise virtue, both as to righteousness towards one another, and piety towards God, and so to come to baptism; for that the washing [with water] would be acceptable to him, if they made use of it, not in order to the putting away of some sins, but for the purification of the body; supposing still that the soul was thoroughly purified beforehand by righteousness. Now when [many] others came in crowds about him, for they were greatly moved by hearing his words. Herod, who feared lest the great influence John had over the people might put it into his power and inclination to raise a rebellion (for they seemed ready to do anything he should advise), thought it best, by putting him to death, to prevent any mischief he might cause, and not bring himself into difficulties, by sparing a man who might make him repent of it when it would be too late. Accordingly he was sent a prisoner, out of Herod's suspicious temper, to Macherus, the castle I before mentioned, and was there put to death. Now the Jews had an opinion that the destruction of this army was sent as a punishment upon Herod, and a mark of God's displeasure to him.[4]

In *Jewish Antiquities* Book 20, Chapter 9, Josephus writes:

...Festus was now dead, and Albinus was but upon the road; so he assembled the sanhedran of judges, and brought before them the brother of Jesus, who was called Christ, whose name was James, and some others; and when he had formed an accusation against them as breakers of the law, he delivered them to be stoned...[5]

Tacitus (c. 55-117 CE) was a Roman senator and historian of the Roman Empire. In *Annals*[6], Book XV he writes:

Consequently, to get rid of the report, Nero fastened the guilt and inflicted the most exquisite tortures on a class hated for their abominations, called Christians by the populace. Christus, from whom the name had its origin, suffered the extreme penalty during the reign of Tiberius at the hands of one of the procurators, Pontius Pilate, and a most mischievous superstition, thus checked for the moment, again broke out not only in Judaea, the first source of the evil, but even in Rome, where all things hideous and shameful from every part of the world find their centre and become popular.[7]

Suetonius (c. 69-140 CE) was a Roman historian in the early Imperial era. He was a close friend of Pliny the Younger[8] and his most important work was a set of biographies of twelve successive Roman rulers from Julius Caesar to Domitian. In *Lives of the Caesars*, Claudius, sec. 25 he writes:

He banished from Rome all the Jews, who were continually making disturbances at the instigation of one

Chrestus [sic].[9]

In *Lives of the Twelve Caesars*, Nero, sec. 16 Suetonius writes:

Punishment was inflicted on the Christians, a class of men given to a new and mischievous superstition.[10]

And so we see that there are various references beyond the biblical ones, but there are overtones that the original writings may have been tampered with, at least to some degree.

NOTES

1. Founded in 1986 on the campus of Willamette University in Salem, Oregon, Westar Institute is 'a member-supported, non-profit research and educational institute dedicated to advancing religious literacy.' http://www.westarinstitute.org/.

2. http://en.wikipedia.org/wiki/Josephus_on_Jesus. Accessed 5 March 2011.

3. Published in Rome in 93 CE but the original manuscripts have been lost. Passages from website as above: http://en.wikipedia.org/wiki/Josephus_on_Jesus.

4. As above. This quotation is considered authentic by *almost* all scholars.

5. As above. Again, this quotation is considered authentic by *almost* all scholars, one reason being that the passage was mentioned in several places by the Egyptian early Christian theologian and scholar Origen (185-254 CE). The phrase 'who was believed to be Christ' is called into dispute as being a Christian insert. Origen clearly states that Josephus remained a conventional Jew all his life and was not a Christian. In his 1991 book, *The Historical*

Jesus: The Life of a Mediterranean Peasant
(Harper One), the Irish-American New
Testatment scholar John Dominic Crossan has
commented on the phrase: 'Josephus' account
is too good to be true, too confessional to be
impartial, too Christian to be Jewish.' Crossan
is a co-founder of the Westar Institute's Jesus
Seminar.
6. Tacitus, Publius (or Gaius) Cornelius, *The
Annals,* BCE 109 trans. Alfred John Church and
William Jackson Brodribb. Online at
http://clasics.nit.edu/Tacitus/annals.html.
7. This massacre ordered by Nero may well
have included Paul in 64 CE among many
other Christians (some would include Peter but
there is very little evidence that Peter was ever
in Rome). The massacre was in response to a
rumour that blamed Nero for a disastrous fire
in Rome. The pejorative language used here
would suggest there has been no tampering
with the original text.
8. Lawyer, author, and magistrate of Ancient
Rome, a writer of letters and prosecutor of
accused Christians.
9. Gaius Suetonius Tranquillus, *Lives of the
Caesars*: *Claudius* (also translated as *Lives of the*

Twelve Caesars) http://www.gutenberg.org/
ebooks/6390.
10. Suetonius, *Lives of the Twelve Caesars: Nero,*
http://www.gutenberg.org/ebooks/6391.

12

Separation of Judaism and Christianity

How and why did Christianity become separated from Judaism? We know that Jesus, Peter and Paul were Jews at their birth, practising Jews all their lives and would have called themselves Jews at their death. They claimed the Torah – the Hebrew scriptures – as their own, although they would have differed with the Rabbis in its interpretation. They all attended the synagogues regularly during their lives and even Paul, in his ministry to the Gentiles, did his proselytizing to those 'God-fearing' Gentiles who regularly attended the synagogue and were accepted by the Jewish community even in their uncircumcised state.

To bring in fresh ideas to this question it is here studied through the eyes of a Jewish writer, Norman Solomon.[1]

[The differences in the interpretation of the Torah] did not become clear until the letters of Paul were written. Up to a certain point in time, perhaps in the middle of the first century – the generation after Jesus – there was no dividing line between Judaism and Christianity. Jesus, indeed, never thought of himself as preaching a religion other than Judaism, or Torah; 'Do

not think I have come to abolish the Law or the Prophets; I have come not to abolish but to fulfil' (Matt. 5:17). If you had asked Jesus or any of his disciples what religion they were, they would have replied 'Jewish'.[2]

It seems to me that the person most responsible for the split from Judaism is Paul, a well educated Pharisee from the diaspora in Tarsus, well versed in Judaism, familiar with the Greek culture, very intelligent, a well trained debater, stubborn, self-opinionated and streets ahead of the uneducated apostles back in Jerusalem, Peter, Jesus brother James and the others. Norman Soloman continues:

The new Testament Book of The Acts of the Apostles, in chapter 15, has preserved an account of an extraordinary confrontation which took place amongst the leaders of the recently formed Christian sect [still synagogue-attending Jews], *probably some time between 50 and 60 CE. By this time Paul...had joined the sect he had previously despised. Together with his friend Barnabas, he returned from Antioch in Syria to canvass support from the Jerusalem leadership for his view that Gentile converts to Christianity need not be circumcised or obey 'the law of Moses'.*

The debate was heated. Whilst Paul and Peter (both themselves Jews) argued that relaxing the strict requirements of the law would make it easier for Gentiles to convert [to this Jewish sect], *others present felt that full commitment to the Torah and its laws was vital. Eventually James, Jesus' brother, proposed* that the burden should not be made too hard, but that Gentiles should at least be required to 'abstain from food polluted by idols, from sexual immorality, from the meat of strangled animals, and from blood' (Acts 15: 20); this compromise, the book relates, was adopted by the gathering, and a letter to that effect dispatched to Antioch, Syria, and Cilicia.

But we know from elsewhere that the compromise was not endorsed by all parties. On the one hand, Paul himself repeatedly declared the 'law of Moses (of which the strangled meat and other prohibitions are part) as obsolete; on the other hand, the 'Jewish Christians', who observed fully the 'Torah of Moses', and who probably included James in their number, flourished for some time and, despite marginalisation by Pauline Christians, continued in their distinct identity for centuries. We can only speculate as to their version of the Jerusalem meeting, for it was the followers of Paul who wrote the New Testament and so shaped later Christianity. History is written by the victors, and in such a way as to justify their interpretation of events.

...This account in Acts highlights some of the factors which sundered apart Jews from emerging Christianity...This was not just a quarrel about doctrine, but a serious social rift. A nation, or religious community, expresses its identity through its laws, customs, and rituals. ...Paul's plan to absorb Gentiles into the community of believers – to 'graft the wild olive' on to the root of the nourishing tree, as he put it (Rom. 11:17) proved incompatible with the way that Jews understood themselves as a people or a community. Instead of uniting 'Jew and Gentile', *it generated two conflicting groups each of which claimed to be the 'true Israel'.*

...The claim that Jesus was the Messiah is not in itself enough to explain the rift; such claims had been made on behalf of others without such far-reaching consequences.

...The destruction of the Jerusalem Temple by the Romans in 70 CE hardened the division and there was no going back. Doctrines hardened on both sides as Christians and Jews defined themselves in opposition to one another.[3]

One could almost say that Paul very much shaped early Christian doctrine, and in his writings he barely refers to the earthly Jesus. His focus is the risen Jesus, the 'Lord' who dwells in the heavens and is present on earth in the Spirit.

To read the new Testament as a whole is thus to be left in no doubt that those who compiled it and deemed it scriptural were the champions of a version of Christianity that wished to stress the divinity of Christ and the almighty power of the God on whose right hand the Son now sits. But there were other options open to those who came in contact with Jesus.

...Those whose views have been recorded – the more educated and philosophical – found the Christian appeal to miracles and resurrection manipulative, the sighing after another world misguided, the worship of a God-man demeaning, and the emphasis on faith irrational.[4]

Would it be an extreme position to suggest that Paul's doctrines made the separation of Christianity from Judaism inevitable and that without his demands for radical concessions to his Gentiles that Christianity could have remained a viable and tolerated sect within Judaism? Certainly some Jewish Christians continued to worship in the synagogues throughout most of the first century and there is evidence that this continued into several centuries thereafter. If Christianity had continued as a branch of Judaism then it would certainly not have appealed to Constantine in his ambitions to form a Church-State alliance and the Church would not have been offered imperial patronage with its enormous financial and legal advantages with the bishops being able to call upon the might of the State to oppose their rivals. How cosy it was for the bishops to wield so much temporal as well as spiritual power being as they were representatives of the earthly as well as the heavenly ruler.

NOTES

> 1. British Orthodox Rabbi, professor and scholar who has been Vice President of the World Congress of Faiths and an Adviser to the International Council of Christians and Jews. His interest 'is in inter-faith dialogue with Christians and Muslims'.
> http://en.wikipedia.org/wiki/
> Norman_Solomon_(rabbi).

2. Norman Solomon, *Judaism: A Very short introduction,* Oxford University Press, London, 1996.

3. ibid., pp. 24-26.

4. Linda Woodhead, *Christianity: A Very short introduction,* Oxford University Press, London, 2004, pp. 15-16.

13

Gnosticism

Why should Gnosticism come in for special attention? In studying first century history this particular group seems to stand out as reflecting what Jesus was really on about. They were not with the winning group when Constantine wanted a uniting religion to help the empire achieve his earthly aspirations in 325 CE so they were among the many losers who were marginalised and declared to be 'heretics'.

The Gnostics believed that Jesus imparted a special wisdom that could help human beings unlock the sacred potential of their own lives. Rather than viewing him as a god who must be worshipped, they viewed him as a divine being who could help individuals get in touch with 'the god within' – the divine potential that lies at the heart of the human.

Gnostic groups existed alongside other forms of early Christianity for several centuries. They wrote gospels (like the Gospel of Thomas), formed canons of scripture, and some developed sophisticated theology that drew on Greek philosophical themes. Where they differed from orthodox Chris-

tianity and its interpretation of Jesus was in their view that human beings were potentially divine. This message had radical, disruptive, and egalitarian possibilities. Later writers attacked the Gnostics for the way in which they treated women as equals, became arrogant with their own knowledge, and threatened to undermine established forms of authority. Recently discovered Gnostic scriptures, most notably from Nag Hammadi in Upper Egypt, reveal that gnosticism drew on female as well as male imagery in speaking of the divine and that it presented Jesus as a teacher who sought not to humble but to exalt his followers. In all respects it challenged the versions of Christianity that found expression in the New Testament and the church that supported it. [1]

The gnostic style of faith is free, open, and creative. One does not have to be told how to act; particularly, what to believe. You have the ability to think for yourself. The gnostic style believes seeking God is more important than finding God by a certain dogma or belief.

Some have estimated that nearly half of early Christians were gnostic in their thinking but the orthodox bishops and Constantine were able to tell the Roman world exactly the correct interpretation of Christ and his intent. The gnostics, who saw the meaning and purpose of Christ differently, were silenced and declared heretics.

The gnostics would seem to have some similarities with the Quakers who have developed a very high doctrine of the Spirit such that they have dispensed with priests, scriptures, and sacraments altogether.

NOTES

1. Linda Woodhead, *Christianity: A Very Short Introduction,* Oxford University Press, London, 2004, pp. 18-19.

14

Contemporary Christian Scholarship

At this stage it would be appropriate to indicate the direction in which contemporary Christian scholarship has been heading in the last twenty years and what conclusions have been reached.

Even if the twenty-first century reconstruction of the historical figure of Jesus turns out to be only partially accurate, I believe it will be nevertheless much closer to the truth than the Jesus of the creeds and the myth of the external Redeemer. Clearly this Jesus of history and the Christ of faith are at loggerheads with each other, the latter being far removed from the world in which twenty-first century *homo sapiens* finds himself. The unchallengeable scientific background provided by Copernicus, Newton, Darwin, Einstein and quantum physics has to be incorporated and accepted as *prima facie* evidence of God's big scheme of things.

Truth and myth were equally accepted as part of life in the first century and the distinctions between the two were blurred. Thus it becomes difficult to distinguish myth from fact in interpreting the synoptic gospels. By general

consensus among modern Christian scholars, it is accepted that Mark was the first gospel, written around seventy
CE following the fall of Jerusalem and some forty years
after the death of Jesus. Paul's letters preceded the gospels
and were written mostly in the fifties before he was put
to death probably in Rome at the hand of Nero in 64 CE.

The next gospels written were Matthew and Luke, about
85 CE. These two writers wrote their gospels independently and had Mark in front of them as they wrote,
together (probably) with another document known
among scholars as 'Q' (this stands for Quelle which is
German for source). 'Q' set out a number of sayings of
Jesus as distinct from details of his doings and was probably written in the fifties, around the same time as Paul's
letters. No copies of this document have been found, but
its contents have been deduced by subtracting Mark from
Matthew and Luke and then setting out which sayings are
common to both Matthew and Luke as distinct from sayings unique to each.[1]

The 'Q' document is in a sense pre-Christian; it is a miss-
ing link between Judaism and Christianity. Jesus in 'Q'
is neither Christ nor the Messiah but rather the last in a
long line of Jewish prophets. These sayings would have
been promulgated in the synagogues not only amongst
the Jews who gathered there but also among God-fearing
Gentiles who came to the synagogues at this time with the
blessing of the Jews. It was among these Gentiles in the
synagogues that Paul found ready acceptance of his message.

The final gospel, that of John, was written about 95 to 100 CE. Contrary to widespread opinion, the authors of all the gospels are unknown. The author of Luke almost certainly wrote The Acts following his gospel, and most scholars, although not all, date the writing of Acts as around 80 CE.

Around 125 CE, at Ephesus, the decision was taken to use all four gospels as the basis for worship. This would keep all aspects of Jesus in perspective and contain any heresies that broke out. It was the early heresies that eventually resulted in the establishment of a canon of works.[2]

Where did the gospel writers source their information? None were eyewitnesses present during Jesus' life nor do they claim to have been except John (John 21: 24). That assertion, however, is simply not supportable with facts. John's was the last gospel to have been written, which means that, if that eyewitness claims were accurate, its author would have been almost 100 years old when he wrote – hardly a possibility in the first century. As former Episcopal Bishop of Newak, New Jersey, and liberal theologian John Shelby Spong notes:

I know of no reputable scholar in the world today who would support the accuracy of the claim that this gospel was the work of that 'beloved disciple'.[3]

Until the gospels were written (in Greek, not Aramaic, which was the language of Jesus), memories were by and large transferred orally. This oral tradition was not put in writing until at least a generation after Jesus' death. The four gospels accepted as canon were not the only ones written at the time but were deemed the only ones doctrinely acceptable by the committees of the evolving church.

Perhaps the most notable omission from the canon is the Gospel of Thomas, an almost complete text of the Coptic translation of this gospel being discovered in Nag Hammadi, Egypt, in 1945. The date of its writing is uncertain, but consensus puts it roughly at the same time as the other gospels. It is a collection of sayings: aphorisms, wisdom sayings, parables, legal and prophetic sayings, all attributed to Jesus. It is not a biography-like gospel and contains almost no biographical material. Roughly half of Thomas's sayings are paralleled independently in the canonical gospels. Significantly 'Q' and Thomas relate no story either of a supernatural birth or a supernatural ascension. There is no account of the crucifixion and no account of the resurrection. There are no parables. There is nothing that presents Jesus in the supernatural theological language that later was to surround him. He presents as a wise teacher and a sage, sometimes even a comic.

Following Jesus' death, his Jewish followers were stunned and sought to find a reason for all that had happened. They began a search of the Jewish scriptures, and by the time the gospels were set down all the biblical references to the Messiah were conjoined to Jesus' life.

Editorial discipline was unknown in the first century and the writers of the gospels had a free hand to add and subtract as they saw fit in order to conform with the evolving theology. This is apparent in comparing the synoptic gospels. At the time of the writing of the synoptic gospels, some generation or more after Jesus' death, it is apparent the embryo church was focussing more on Jesus himself than on his teachings. Jesus' humanity faded with each evolutionary step, whilst his divinity increased. Thus the gospel writers took liberties and were not averse to making their own additions to make Jesus' life coincide with Old Testament predictions of the Messiah or even creating their individual accounts of parts of Jesus' life to make the story fit what they believed He was on about.

One should at this point touch briefly upon modern neuro-psychological concepts of memory and the understanding of the fallibility of eyewitness accounts. Modern research indicates that eyewitness memory, and remember here in the first century we are referring to an interlude of several decades, is not nearly as reliable nor as accurate as widely believed. Two common errors in thinking that contribute to this situation are the hindsight bias and overconfidence effects. The hindsight bias is the tendency to reshape one's interpretation of the past to fit in with known outcomes. The subject is not deliberately nor consciously being fraudulent but their recall is at variance with the actual event.

As early as 1896 Freud observed that memories are not written down once, or 'engraved', to remain unchanged forever, but can be altered by subsequent events and retranscribed. Freud further observed that events could take on an altered meaning for patients years after they occurred, and that patients then altered their memories of those events.[4]

In trying to sift out what Jesus actually said, scholars are guided by two characteristics which were unique to his teaching. He taught in parables and aphorisms (pithy one-line sayings). In his teaching he did not involve himself in long monologues, and where these occur in the gospels doubts should arise.

A parable empowers rather than dominates an audience. It challenges them to think and judge for themselves. It is the most appropriate teaching technique for a Kingdom of God in which God empowers rather than dominates, challenges rather than controls.[5]

Jesus' impressionistic canvas is offered so that people in their individual settings can complete the painting in a style appropriate to their own circumstances.

One should not forget that in the Greek and Roman world of deities of the first century competition was intense. Anybody that was anybody had to have at least one supernatural parent, and naturally enough the recipients of such claims never denied them. Julius Caesar claimed descent from the goddess Venus, daughter of Jupiter. Alexander the Great's mother Olympias had supposedly been impregnated by a god, and even more recently Emperor Hirohito, the WWII emperor of Japan, claimed descent from the sun goddess Amaterasu. Thus it was completely acceptable by the populace at large, or even mandatory, that if Jesus were to compete on even terms with, say, Caesar, then he had to have at least one divine parent. Christianity had to be competitive in the Hellenistic culture.

What does the reading of Paul contribute to the differential diagnosis? Paul's writings predate the first synoptic gospel by probably some twenty years. They were written between 50 CE and 64 CE.

Paul was a Jew, a Pharisee from Tarsus, and he comes across as being well-educated and more than a match for the Jerusalem church of Peter and Jesus' brother James, with whom he had an early disputation on circumcision. His letters are fluent and plausible and his influence in the developing church has been profound. In fact the theology of the Protestant churches seems based on his doctrines in contrast with the Catholic Church which is based more on the gospels.

In Paul there is no reference to a miraculous birth; Jesus was 'born of a woman, born under the law' (Gal.4:4). There is no hint of the concept of virginity. In this, the twenty-first century, theologians should be asking what was the genetic disposition of Jesus at His conception? What was the disposition of the XY chromosome from the Holy Spirit and did Mary contribute the XX chromosome which would have been imperfect?

There are no miracle stories anywhere in the writings of Paul. A Roman citizen and a Pharisee, he remained proud of those facts throughout his life. In contrast to the Sadducees, the Pharisees believed in the resurrection, so it was no huge jump in his theology for Paul to proclaim Jesus' resurrection to become the Son of God (Romans 1:1-4). There is no indication in Paul's writing that his understanding of the resurrection was that of a physical resurrection (1 Cor. 15:35-55). In support of this understanding Paul lists his own conversion experience as a resurrection experience not unlike all the other resurrection appearances that he describes (1 Cor. 15:1-10).

There is in Paul no mention of an empty tomb, suggesting that the empty-tomb story is not known to him or was a later addition. Interestingly, Paul does not focus on Jesus' teachings or His life in any of his writings, as though they are of no importance. Accordingly, we get no help from Paul in our quest for the historical Jesus. In Paul there is, however, very little of the theistic framework and very little of the imposed supernaturalism that was to develop later.

Some forty years later, as the church cemented its theology at the end of the first century, John changed the timing of the deification of Jesus to predate his birth: '...the Word was made flesh' (John 1:14). And so we see in the evolving theology of the church the humanity of Jesus very much playing second fiddle to his alleged divinity throughout his life.

No essay of this nature would be complete without alluding to the Protestant emphasis on sin. God is good and hence would not deliberately create an evil world. However, some writers in the Hebrew Bible – the author of

Job, for example – attribute both good and evil to the same God. One of the most forceful articulations of evil is found in Dostoevsky's *The Brothers Karamozov*, in which Ivan complains to his brother Alyosha that he cannot understand how the world will ever find the harmony of a divinely ordained reconciliation of evil with good.[6] The sufferings of a child for the sake of creation will cry out for all eternity.

St. Augustine (354-430 CE) came to believe that God had condemned humankind to eternal damnation all because of Adam's original sin. This 'inherited sin' was passed on through what Augustine called concupiscence, the desire to take pleasure in sex rather than God. From Augustine on, Christians viewed humanity as chronically flawed.[7] Well, Augustine may perhaps have felt the guilt of the hedonistic lifestyle he led as a young priest, having a lover as he did for thirteen years and fathering a son. No wonder he is famous for his prayer, 'Grant me chastity and continence, Oh Lord, but not yet!'[8]

All the church fathers and most of the Protestant reformers stressed that humankind was in a state of rebellion (sin) over which we have no control. Because of sin, the reformers taught, people are estranged from the divine. They are so corrupt and unacceptable to God that they are incapable of doing anything to redeem their status. Especially, they cannot reason their way into the good graces of the divine.

The University of Chicago's Professor of Theological

Ethics, William Schweiker, made the points below in a
series of discussions following the 2001 terror attacks on
New York city:

*There are those in each tradition who argue that human rea-
son is so distorted or so feeble or so impotent that we cannot
ever make valid moral judgements about how to live rightly.
Given that, we must utterly submit all thinking to those who
claim rightly to interpret the decisive revelation of God's will...*

*Within ultraconservative Roman Catholicism... one must sub-
mit to the infallible teaching of the papacy and magisterium.
Within fundamentalist Protestantism...this means an attack
on all human inquiry and the demand for complete submission
to a literal reading of the Bible. These kinds of revelation-
ism...are the backbone of fanatical and authoritarian movements around the world and within each of these traditions.*[9]

This attempt to discredit the human mind has, unfortunately, put the church at war with its own tradition.

*Wisdom is an important part of the old testament under-
standing of God*[10]*...Wisdom is considered a part of the divine
nature.*

*...Ultimately, the argument that reason is a hindrance to faith
dies by falling on its own sword. All negative conclusions are
reached through logical processes. The advocates of this position find themselves in an embarrassing position. They have*

used reason to conclude that reason is too sinful to be helpful. That bird will not fly![11]

It would seem to me that often when a reasonable question is raised concerning a doctrinal point, the standard response is that the answer is beyond the ken of human understanding, and that ends any debate.

Toronto Minister and founder of the Canadian Center for Progressive Christianity, Gretta Vosper:

Having an open mind within the church has been rather unnecessary for most of Christendom. Everything we've ever needed to know has come to us through the 'proper' channels, with a few breaks from the norm down through the ages. A quick scramble for the keys to the kingdom and their inherent power over determining just what it was that we needed to know took place in the early days of the church. But there were so many apologists, each of whom was cast by the other as heretics, that it was actually Constantine's councils, not Jesus, that granted those powerful keys to a group that eagerly claimed them. Since that time, the church, with amazing consistency, has masterfully engineered, managed, and controlled its doctrine. Given that it hasn't changed much since then, it has been what some would call an easy job.

With the church having been made the repository of the truth, and claiming the right and authority to interpret the Bible in the pursuit of that truth, there was little anyone needed to think about. Where to take your burning questions was very clear: if you dared, you went to those who, in the appropriate ecclesiastical garb, could answer them. And you believed every word they said.

If you didn't believe what they said, you could doubt. The faithful have always doubted. But you didn't say much about it, and you certainly didn't argue publicly against what the church said. To present or profess a different understanding could easily lead one to be excommunicated...This might not seem a very big deal. For those within the Roman Catholic Church, however, it is still a very big deal indeed...Excommunication means eternal banishment.

...For most of Christendom, outside the church there has been no mortal peace either. Heretics, those who would put forward a version of reality that was inconsistent with that presented by the church, could be disciplined, imprisoned, killed, or forced to recant heretical beliefs through any number of creative ways, some of which continue to be used to this day for political purposes.

...You need to be able to critique what you hold in your head. Ideas that have been offered to you are just that, ideas. They are malleable. They can be shifted around, stewed over, seen from different angles. They are mere food for thought. Your own thought. The church has worked very hard to hold on to their responsibility to do that for you. Take it back. [12]

It is interesting to follow the conditioning mechanism

that the church has skilfully developed over many centuries. Vosper sets this out lucidly:

Throughout the school years, the child continues to check its place against those in authority, usually parents, but increasingly institutional leaders and peers. Each time he or she checks, the push to conform is reinforced. Thus does the child, by the time adulthood is reached...have each belief integrated into the reality of the young adult's life. He or she has learned how to express it, how to live it out, and how to affirm it when seen in others ...Here is where conventional beliefs become the norm...What he or she believes is straightforward, unchallenged, and simply there...Questions are unnecessary and, in all likelihood, not even raised.

Many who live in this stage remain in it until they die. Their belief system, perfectly laid out to handle any of life's big questions, is sufficient for them, no matter what happens. Very little can shake it... Remaining committed to their beliefs despite what happens is applauded by the community as a sign of a strong and true faith.

When you walk into a church, the community that gathers is all about reinforcing beliefs. We might even say that this is the chief purpose of Sunday morning services – to reinforce the belief systems that are assimilated at an early age by most Christians. Language, behaviours, readings, symbols, are all geared to this purpose.[13]

Don Cupitt, former Dean of Emmanuel College, Cambridge, who has a strong following in modern Christian scholarship, affirms this line of thinking in setting out his 'Creed':

Article 2 is about owning one's life, which means both acknowledging it, and assuming full responsibility for planning and running it. You are *your own life. Your personal identity is not a secret thing hidden inside you: it is your life and the roles you play...*

...Here I reject the traditional idea that there is great virtue in obedience to religious law and to the direction of religious superiors. Instead I join all those young people who would rather die than put up with an arranged marriage, or any career or life-path chosen for them by someone else. In traditional Christianity the demand for personal religious freedom has always been condemned as deeply sinful, but I think we must now insist upon it. One must choose one's own life, both making it one's own and seeking fully to express oneself in it. One must come out in one's own life.[14]

I can no longer hold in good conscience that God delivered Jesus up to death for our sake as a sacrifice for our sins, or that his death in itself has any saving significance. The whole concept I find totally abhorrent and barbaric.

Retired New Jersey Methodist Minister and theological scholar Theodore J. Weeden, a member of the Jesus Seminar at the Westar Insitute[15]:

For all this, Christian Orthodoxy is almost solely indebted to Paul, the first expositor of the cult of the dying and rising saviour from which the church has never deviated...in my judgement, from its earliest days Christian Orthodoxy's establishing of the New Testament canon and its creedal formations has almost completely misrepresented Jesus and the intent of his life and mission. The Sayings Gospel Q which originated as early as the late 30s or 40s CE, long before Matthew, Mark, Luke and John, presents a radically different view of the life and significance of Jesus. Along with other early manuscripts, the Gospel of Mary, the Gospel of Thomas and the Didache, a first-century church manual, contrary to the Pauline tradition and the canonical gospels, they show no interest in Jesus' death and resurrection per se, but focus instead on applying Jesus' life and teaching to the purpose of realising God's kingdom in this life. [16]

I do not hold to the opinion that Jesus historically viewed himself as the Messiah or Son of God, nor do I believe that he held any other exalted understanding of himself, nor perceived God to have bestowed on him any elevated status.

Where do we stand in regard to miracles? A miracle is a violation of the laws of nature, and therefore could only be performed by God or those God has entrusted with divine powers. David Hume, the Scottish Philosopher quoted in Chapter 5, lists in his 1748 treatise *An Enquiry concerning human understanding* (Section X: Of

Miracles)[17] the ways in which human beings lack complete reliability:

People are prone to accept the unusual and incredible, which excite agreeable passions and wonder

Those with strong religious beliefs are often prepared to give evidence that they know to be false 'with the best intentions in the world, for the sake of promoting so holy a cause'

People are often too credulous when faced with such witnesses, whose apparent honesty and eloquence (together with the psychological effects of the marvellous) may overcome normal scepticism

The history of every culture displays a pattern of development from a wealth of supernatural events which steadily decreases over time, as the culture grows in knowledge and understanding of the world.[18]

The experience of most of us is that we have never come remotely close to what we would call a miracle, nor have we spoken with anyone who has made such a claim, or at least anyone whose testimony we would deem reliable. In the medical profession most of us have encountered cancers that have been advanced, and then for some seemingly inexplicable reason, resolve and disappear. Such was the case with Mary Mackillop when it was claimed by the Congregation for the Causes of Saints that Veronica Hopson was cured of leukaemia in 1961 by dint of her praying to Mary Mackillop for her intercession[18]. The second accepted miracle was that of Kathleen Evans, who, in the 1990s was said to have been cured of inoperable lung cancer with brain secondaries.[19] As a result a papal decree was issued and Mary Mackillop's beatification took place. Well deserved no doubt but, in my opinion, not because of the so-called miracles.

It is my firm opinion based on a lifetime of surgical experience, dealing widely with cancers of many organs, that spontaneous resolution of advanced cancers does occur naturally but on very rare occasions; not because of the prayers or petitions of the patient or their loved ones but because of some so-far unexplained medical phenomenon. It may well be that on very rare occasions the body's immune system responds favourably but at a late stage to some structure in the cancer cell and is able to destroy each and every cell. More commonly one has seen patients whose body somehow enters a symbiosis with their advanced cancer and the inevitable advance towards death halts and the patient may carry on for many more years with the cancer not resolving but its usual inexorable advance becoming static.

One wonders at the competence of those who comprise the Congregation for the Causes of Saints. Or is it to do with integrity, motives and power structure?...A wise man proportions his belief to the evidence.

David Hume
Of Miracles (1748)[12]

NOTES

1. Marcus Borg, *The Lost Gospel Q,* Ulysses
Press, Berkeley, 1999.
2. Peter Watson, *Ideas: A History from fire to
Freud,* Phoenix Paperback, London, 2006, p.
311
3. John Shelby Spong, *Liberating the Gospels:
reading the Bible with Jewish eyes*, Harper
Collins, New York, 1997, p. 68.
4. J. M. Mason, Ed. and transl., *The Complete
Letters of sigmund Freud to Wilhelm Fliess,*
Harvard University Press, Cambridge, 1985, p.
207.
5. John Dominic Crossan and Richard G. Watts
(Ed.) *Who is Jesus?*, Harper Collins/Westminster
John Knox Press, Louisville, 1996, p. 51.
6. Malcolm V. Jones and Garth M. Terry, *New
Essays on Dostoyevsky*, Cambridge University
Press, Cambridge, 1983. p. 27.
7. Peter Watson, op. cit., p. 316.
8. In the supplement to Third Part of his
Summa Theologica, St Thomas Aquinas replies
to a question about the relations of the saints
towards the damned:

9. *Wherefore in order that the happiness of the saints may be more delightful to them and that they may render more copious thanks to God for it, they are allowed to see perfectly the sufferings of the damned.*

10. Online at:

11. http://www.gutenberg.org/ebooks/1995 and http://www.newadvent.org/summa/ 5094.htm. Accessed 27 May 2013.

12. William Schweiker, 'The Intellectual's Responsibility and the Ambiguity of the Religions of the Book, part II: A Shared Pattern of Moral Conviction', *Sightings,* University of Chicago, 24 October, 2001. http://divinity.uchicago.edu/martycenter/ publications/sightings/archive_2001/ sightings-102401.shtml

13. John C. Polkinghorne paraphrased in Jack Good, *The Dishonest Church,* Saint Johann Press, 2008, p. 101.

14. Jack Good, ibid.

15. Gretta Vosper, *With or without God,* Harper Perennial, New York, 2009, pp. 159-161.

16. ibid., pp. 262-263.

17. Don Cupitt, *The Future of the Christian tradition,* Polebridge Press, Salem 2007, p. 128.

18. As noted in Chaper 8: Founded in 1986 on
the campus of Willamette University in Salem,
Oregon, Westar Institute is 'a member-
supported, non-profit research and
educational institute dedicated to advancing
religious literacy.'
http://www.westarinstitute.org/.
19. Theodore J. Weeden in Charles W. Hedrick
(Ed.) *When faith meets reason,* Polebridge Press,
Salem, 2008, p. 93.
20. David Hume, *Enquiries concerning human
understanding,* Ed. L. A. Selby-Bigge, 3rd ed.
revised P. H. Nidditch. Clarendon Press,
Oxford, 1975, p.93. Online at
21. http://www.catholic.org/saints/
saint.php?saint_id=4958
22. http://www.marymackillop.org.au/
canonisation/index.cfm?loadref=62
23. David Hume, *An Enquiry concerning human
understanding,* Section X: Of Miracles, Harvard
Classics Vol. 37, P. F Collier & Son, 1910.
Online at http://18th.eserver.org/hume-
enquiry.html#10

15

A Profile of the Historical Jesus

Having now assembled an assortment of 'clinical' evidence, albeit very brief, we could set out some conclusions (personal) on the profile of the historical Jesus.

- He was born around 0-5 BCE in Nazareth, not Bethlehem, by normal birth. The virginal conception of Jesus is later faith in Jesus retrojected mythologically onto Jesus as an infant.[1] His birth was not heralded by wise men, angels, or shepherds.
- He was a Galilean Jew at birth and at death.
- He was a tekton (carpenter). This occupation indicated that his predecessors had been dispossessed of land and consequently he belonged to a lower social stratum in Galilee. He would have been well aware of economic hardship and social division.[2]
- He had four brothers, James, Joseph, Simon and Judas and at least two sisters (Matthew

13:55). James may well have been the eldest in the family given his prominence in a leadership position later in Jerusalem after Jesus' death.

- Cross-cultural anthropology would suggest that Jesus was illiterate, since between ninety-five and ninety-seven per cent of the Jewish state was illiterate at the time of Jesus. As He would have been aware of the oral culture and basic stories but not the exact texts. Crotty, in his *Three Revolutions,* states bluntly: 'The gospel texts must be seen for what they are: Lukan propaganda.'[3]

- He was baptised in the Jordan by John the Baptist and was influenced by his teaching.

- Around the age of thirty he chose an unknown number of apostles and moved around Judea.

- He belonged to the wisdom tradition of Israel[4] – along with Job, Proverbs, Ecclesiates, and the Wisdom of Solomon. Wisdom is not concerned with theories of sin and salvation, but how to cope with life. He is identified as a mystic rather than as a lawgiver or a prophet.

- He did not declare any intention of starting a new religion or even another version of Judaism. He emphasised certain aspects of his Jewish faith as true spirituality.'

- He wrote nothing that we know of and we cannot know with any degree of certainty whether we are hearing the words of a person named Jesus or the collected thoughts of the early church based around a person named Jesus.
- He was an exorcist but not a worker of miracles. There are no historical records of Jesus' miracles only the words of those who *believed* he was the Messiah or Son of God.
- He taught by way of parables and aphorisms.

Jesus Seminar's Mahlon H. Smith:

Not only could the historical Jesus not have uttered many of the claims ascribed to him in the gospel of John (such as John 10: 30, and most of the 'I am' sayings), it is highly unlikely that he would have approved of the general tendency of Christians to elevate him to the status of sole mediator of divine authority.[5]

- His teachings were that heaven is here on earth in the here and now.

The Gospel of Thomas (Nag Hammadi documents[6]) No. 3:

Jesus said...If those who lead you, say to you, 'See the kingdom is in the sky,' then the birds of the sky will precede you. If they

say to you, 'It is in the sea,' then the fish will precede you.
Rather the kingdom is inside of you, and it is outside of you.[7]

Interestingly the Pope puts a completely different interpretation on this concept, maintaining that the kingdom
is Jesus himself.[8]

- He was fully human and not divine.
- He was seen as a threat to Roman Imperialism,
  a troublemaker who criticised Jewish religion
  and argued with Jewish teachers. His public
  career was viewed as threatening the peace of
  the Roman Province of Palestine. He was killed
  by the Romans, probably crucified but this is
  uncertain.
- Jesus' first followers knew almost nothing
  whatsoever about the details of his crucifixion,
  death, or burial. What we have now in those
  detailed passion accounts is not 'history
  remembered' but 'prophecy historicised'[9] as
  his followers searched the Jewish scriptures
  after his death.
- No physical resurrection took place.
- The only historical kernels behind the gospel
  events from Palm Sunday to Easter morn are
  Jesus' provocative act against the Temple
  money-changers and Jesus' crucifixion.[10]

- There was no ascension in any literal sense into a heaven located somewhere above the sky.
- There is no evidence that Jesus founded a church or established an ecclesiastical hierarchy.
- There is no evidence that he created sacraments as a special means of Grace.
- He did not teach that human beings are born in sin and that, unless baptised, they will be forever banished from God's presence.
- He did teach of the

...ironic nature of God who sometimes motivates even those like the despised Samaritan to do good while those who are concerned for religious purity pass by on the other side. He encouraged others to see themselves as offspring of the Creator of the universe and therefore worthy to appeal to their cosmic parent directly rather than through him or any other religious mediator.[11]

- His life, his teachings and his presence had a permanent magnetic effect on all those with whom he came in contact, and for many ever since, this response has been ongoing. This cannot be ignored.

It is ironic to realise that the religion that formed

around Jesus would within four hundred years begin
to claim for itself an institutional monopoly on grace
and access to God.
Marcus J. Borg
The Heart of Christianity [12]

NOTES

1. John Dominic Crossan, *Jesus: A Revolutionary
biography,* Harper Collins, New York, 1994. p.
23.

2. Crotty, Robert, *Three revolutions: three drastic
changes in interpreting the Bible*, ATF Theology
Press, Adelaide, 2012. pp. 200-201.

3. ibid., pp. 25-26.

4. An entire portion of Jewish scripture is
known as wisdom literature. This includes
Psalms, Proverbs, Ecclesiastes, Lamentations
and portions of other books.

5. Mahlon H. Smith in Charles W. Hedrick
(ed.), *When faith meets reason,* Polebridge Press,
Salem, 2008, p. 76.

6. Refer Chapter 12, p. 68.

7. Gerd Luedemann in Spong, John Shelby;
Borg, Marcus and Funk, Robert W. et al. *The
Once and future Jesus*, Polebridge Press, Salem,
2000, pp.151-152. Also online at

http://gnosis.org/naghamm/gthlamb.html.
Accessed 26 May 2013.
8. Joseph Ratzinger, *Jesus of Nazareth*,
Bloomsbury, London, 2007, p. 60.
9. John Dominic Crossan, op. cit., p. 145.
10. Theodore J. Weedon in Charles W. Hedrick
(ed.), *When faith meets reason,* Polebridge Press,
Salem, 2008, p. 84.
11. Mahlon H. Smith, op. cit., p. 80.
12. Marcus J. Borg, *The Heart of Christianity,*
Harper Collins, New York, 1989. p. 41.

16

The Formation of the Early Church

After Jesus was killed, many diverse 'Jesus movements' sprang up, each group having its own characteristics and following what they felt Jesus' teachings meant. One group followed the more traditional Jewish codes of ethics and from this group came communities that lasted for centuries, such as the Ebionites and the Nazarines. The Ebionites rejected the doctrines espoused by Paul. These groups were not the ones that gave birth to the Christianity of the Bible. Another line followed on from the Sayings Gospel Q^1, runs through the Gospel of Thomas where Jesus teachings were understood to bring enlightenment about one's true self, and ends up in Gnostic circles.

US author and scholar of early Christian studies Burton L. Mack tracks the emergence of the Church:

This approach may have been the most attractive form of Christianity during the second to fourth centuries. It was finally squelched by the institutional form of Christian tradi-

*tion that called itself the universal church and labelled all oth-
er followers of Jesus heretics.*[2]

Many other Jesus movements developed in these early
times and included the True Disciples who produced the
Gospel of Thomas, the Congregation of Israel and the
Jerusalem Pillars about whom Paul speaks in his letter to
the Galations. Each of these groups differs from the others in important ways but all of them considered Jesus the
founder of their movement.

Mack again:

*The road from Jesus to the Christian religion finally emerged
in the fourth century, with its myth of Jesus as the son of God
solidly in place, is a very long and twisty path. Christianity
was not born of an immaculate conception. It was the product
of myriad moments of intellectual labour and negotiated social
agreements by the people investing in the experiment.*

*This discovery has been difficult for many Christians to
accept. That is because the traditional picture of Christian
beginnings starts with a Jesus who knows in advance what
is required of him and his disciples in order to establish the
Christian religion. The way Luke tells the story in his two vol-
ume history of Christian origins, for instance, is that after his
death but before his ascension Jesus announced the establishment of the First Christian Church of Jerusalem by means of
the outpouring of God's Spirit on the day of Pentecost (Acts
1-2). We now know that Luke wrote his gospel and the Acts*

of the Apostles in the early second century, seventy five or more years after the time of Jesus, and that he had reasons for wanting to imagine things that way ... There is not a trace of evidence in any of the early Jesus materials to support such a view. No early Jesus group thought of Jesus as the Christ or of itself as a Christian church.[3]

What about the historical Jesus? The first followers of Jesus were not interested in preserving accurate memories of the historical person. Jesus was important to them as the founder/teacher of a school of thought. His importance as a thinker and teacher can be greatly enhanced once we allow the thought that Jesus was not a god incarnate but a real historical person.

The Sayings Gospel Q brings the early Jesus people into focus. Instead of people meeting to worship a risen Christ, as in the Pauline congregations, or worrying about what it meant to be a follower of a martyr, as in the Markan community, the people of Q were fully preoccupied with questions about the kingdom of God in the present and the behaviour required, if one took it seriously.

The 'pillars' in Jerusalem comprised a group of Galileans including the apostles Peter, James and John. They remained distinctly Jewish in their ideas and practices including purity codes but were by and large too dense to get the picture of the kingdom Jesus painted. It was only in Matthew's gospel (about 85 CE) that they were rehabilitated in Matthew's reconstructed history. Paul had a rather adversarial meeting with them in the late fifties but by and large little is known of this Jerusalem group. They were probably swept away with the fall of Jerusalem in 70 CE or fled to Pella. Any remnants would have certainly have been eliminated in the Simon bar Kokhbar revolt of 135 CE. It is most unlikely that Peter ever travelled to Rome as mythologised by the Roman church. They were certainly not a 'Christian' congregation of the Pauline type and in all likelihood disappeared into oblivion.

Burton Mack hones in on a pivotal change in belief that converted one of these Jesus movements into the Christ cult:

Beginning somewhere in northern Syria, probably in the city of Antioch, and spreading through Asia minor into Greece, one of these Jesus movements underwent a change of historic consequence. It was a change that turned a Jesus movement into a cult of a god called Jesus Christ. At first sight it is difficult to imagine that the Christ cult was at one time a Jesus movement, for the change was so drastic and appears to have happened so suddenly.

The Christ cult differed from the Jesus movements in two major respects. One was the focus upon the significance of Jesus' death and destiny...this focus on Jesus' death had the result of shifting attention away from the teachings of Jesus and away from a sense of belonging to his school. It engendered instead an elaborate preoccupation with notions of martyrdom, resurrection, and the transformation of Jesus into a divine, spiritual presence. The other major difference was the forming of a cult orientated to that spiritual presence. Hymns, prayers, acclamations, and doxologies were composed when Christians met together in Jesus' name. These features are distinctive and mark the Christ cult as strikingly different from all the other Jesus movements.

Evidence for the Christ cult comes mainly from the letters of Paul written during the 50s...The Christ people must have been making their presence felt in a way that aroused Paul's hostility when first he encountered them. And yet, they must have been attractive enough to have occasioned his later conversion...Because these people were the first ones who used the term Christ when referring to Jesus, we may think of them as the first Christians.

...Making the claim that a mixed group of Jesus people represented God's plan for restructuring human society was not a simple matter. An elaborate mythology was developed which was rooted in the logic of martyrdom, or the Greek tradition of the noble death, but it drew as well on a number of other myths that were current at the time. These included a Jewish wisdom tale about the vindication of a falsely charged righteous man, the Greek concepts of hero and divine man, ancient Near Eastern myths of the king as God's son, and the story of Israel as a people who lived constantly under the eye of God...The process of merging myths to create new symbols was standard practice [in the Greco-Roman age].[4]

Paul took the ball and ran with it enthusiastically! Paul was converted to a Jesus movement that had already become a congregation of the Christ. When the Jesus people first entertained the Christ myth, it was not intended as a proclamation to the rest of the world. To Paul, however, his conversion was construed by him as a call to become a missionary for this new gospel. It would solve a social issue for Jewish synagogues in the diaspora by turning their situation into a historic opportunity for the glory of Israel's God.

Paul's missionary path was not all straight forward. At times he formulated doctrine 'on the run'. This was apparent in his early letter to the Galatians in answer to their question on what happened to the Christians that had died. Paul gets involved in a bizarre exercise of illogical gymnastics ending up with the dead and the living meeting the Lord 'in the clouds'. What an astounding imagination! We can almost see Paul desperately trying to work it out on the spot. The doctrine ends as Paul says 'in the air'.

The next tangle Paul gets himself into is trying to reconcile Gentiles with Jews. With another gymnastic turn of logic in his letter to the Galations he suggests Gentiles could claim to have a Jewish connection by virtue of Jesus being the 'seed' of Abraham and therefore through him all Gentiles could claim the blessing of God. Paul gave little thought as to what his fellow Jews would think of his preposterous reasoning but at all events in later epistles he seems to go cool on this weird idea which formed part of his myth making strategy.

There is no doubt that Paul, having put his signature to so many preserved letters outlining his theological doctrines, played the major role in creating a foundation on which the Christian religion rested.

Despite the persecution of the Christian Church during the first three centuries, it prospered and grew. Its future was assured when Constantine became the sole Roman Emperor in 324 CE and gave his full support to the Christian Church as the church of the empire. He commanded the Christian bishops to meet in Nicaea and to unify their doctrines and appointed Eusebius to decide on books to be included in sacred scriptures. He wanted 50 copies for the new churches he planned to build in Constantinople. As it transpired, the debate about which books were to be included and which were not to be included continued for some centuries. Certainly all the writings of the marginalised Jesus people were destroyed.

The Christ cult thus received Royal patronage and became rich and powerful, a position it maintains today.

NOTES

1. Q being the 'Gospel of Jewish Christianity', which continued in Galilee to proclaim Jesus' sayings, with 'The Sayings Gospel Q' an archaic collection of sayings ascribed to Jesus.
2. Burton L. Mack, *Who wrote the New Testament?,* Harper Collins, New York, 1989, p. 41.
3. ibid., p. 45.
4. ibid., pp. 75-76.

17

The Spirit Behind the Universe

Who has seen the wind
Neither I nor you
But when the leaves hang trembling
The wind is passing thro'

Who has seen the wind?
Neither you nor I:
But when the trees bow down their heads
The wind is passing by.

Christina Rossetti[1]

A more difficult task at this juncture is to come to conclusions about the nature of any spirit behind the workings of the universe. One hesitates to relate his presence to homo sapiens as that would seem to be the height of arrogance, taking on the assumption that man deserves any greater attention than the least of his creations.

In the final analysis, the conclusions reached on the evidence set out makes a working 'diagnosis' nigh on impossible. We are left with rather a 'differential diagnosis' based on the footprints we find all around us.

One conclusion we come to in following the logic set out above is that the 'Master of the Universe' is immanent. In other words, he pervades the whole universe and maintains the laws of physics on line so that chaos can never take over. It does not necessarily follow that there is complete rigidity in the system but evolution in this system occurs and is subject to chance, as we have learned. The evolutionary time frame for any change is almost beyond our comprehension, being measured as it is in millions of years rather than the three score and ten of our brief sojourn. Does this immanence hold true on a molecular or atomic or even subatomic level? I suppose the answer has to be yes to be consistent, even though it is hard to wrap one's mind around this concept.

Brian Swimme made a contribution to this idea when he wrote:
[The evolutionary process] is really simple. Here's the whole story in one line. This is the greatest discovery of the scientific enterprise: you take hydrogen gas, and you leave it alone, and it turns into rose bushes, giraffes, and humans.
That's the short version. The reason I like that version is that hydrogen gas is odourless and colourless, and in the prejudice of our western civilisation, we see it as just material stuff. There's not much there. You just take hydrogen, leave it alone, and it turns into a human – that's a pretty interesting bit of information. The point is that if humans are spiritual, then hydrogen's spiritual. It's an incredible opportunity to escape the traditional dualism – you know, the spirit is up there; matter is down here. Actually, it's different. You have the matter

*all the way through, and so you have the spirit all the way
through. So that's why I love the short version.*[2]

Pretty persuasive stuff!
Does this mean that this 'Spirit' of the universe is not
transcendent, that he does not exist beyond the physical
universe? That is a mystery. Sometimes in Medicine one
has to go on 'gut feelings.' My gut feeling is that this Spirit
is transcendent, existing somewhere beyond our senses
and not confined to the universe.

Is the 'Spirit' behind the universe immutable? Traditional
teaching has it that he is unchangeable. Again a subject
of delightful ponderings into the unknown, but if this
spirit is part of the evolutionary process in partnership
with his creation, then the possibility exists that he is
not immutable. But then again, if he is beyond time and
space (as well as within time and space), he is probably
immutable. Surely something in this changing stormy
environment in which we find ourselves must constitute
a solid safe anchorage.

Some authors, such as the Jesus Seminar's historian
Charles Hedrick, disagree with the above reasoning and
perhaps next year I shall too:
*I do not think God is coequal with nature (pantheism), and I do
not find God in nature (panentheism). The natural order has
neither conscience nor morals, so how can it 'reflect' God?...I
find that I can learn very little about the nature or character
of God from the natural world.*[3]

Accepting the tenor of the arguments above, one finds oneself with a very impersonal deity and a very incomplete picture, a problem with which the author of the previous paragraph grapples. And, of course, this does not coincide with personal experience. This gap seems to be naturally filled by the persona of Jesus and all he aspired to and taught during his lifetime. This is the Jesus of history, not the Christ of faith. To me the Jesus of history has been misrepresented by the traditional church and usurped to be put in a position that he never intended nor sought. His essential humanity and humility could never be replicated in the dual role of 'truly human, truly God.'

There would seem to be no doubt that the Jesus of history is the inspiration for man for all time and transmits all the desirable characteristics that each one of us would aspire to but never acquires. One is drawn to the inescapable conclusion that the human being in the form of Jesus had qualities that reach closest to our ideal of a perfect life, one not lived with the expectation of a reward at the end.

So far there has been no mention of prayer. Is it useful; is it a waste of time? We have discarded the notion of a grey-bearded old man being inundated with petitions at a frightening rate. Of course in the freeze-frame concept of time developed above there could be all the time in the world to deal with each prayer individually. But this is a ridiculous concept. The facts as they stand suggest that God chooses not to interfere in the daily events and chooses not to answer petitions no matter how overwhelming the avalanche. The bitter experience of the Holocaust led many to deny the traditional concept of an 'interventionist' God; God had evidently not intervened in response to the prayers of his people to save them from this terrible catastrophe. Well, is it all then a waste of time? This would not seem to be the experience of mortal man.

My own bush theology would suggest that we address prayers to the spirit within each of us. There is no magic transmission through the ether to an old man with his ear bent towards us. These prayers are answered in turn by a suggested alteration to our own personal attitudes and response to the particular situation in which we find ourselves. For example, we may have a sick friend. Our prayer frees our mind of all the extraneous day-to-day thoughts and focuses on that particular friend and moulds our response to his or her situation. We may resolve to pay them a visit or take them some food. Our prayer to the Spirit within us (some would say conscience) empowers us to do the job ourselves and fulfil our obligations with no expectation that the Almighty will wave a wand and make that friend better. Having said that, what about public prayers pronounced by a designated leader? My personal response has always been one of discomfort: it seems to me to be pretentious and ostentatious, focusing more on the leader's intonations and language than any Almighty listener.

Founder of the Jesus Seminar, Robert Funk[4] discusses the group's response to the New Testament's recipe for prayer:
And when you pray, don't act like phonies. They love to stand

up and pray in houses of worship and on street corners, so they
can show off in public. ...When you pray, go into a room by
yourself and shut the door behind you...
(Matthew 6, 5-6)

Surprisingly, twenty-seven per cent of the eminent scholars of the Jesus Seminar thought this passage did not go
back to Jesus at all but was a gospel editorial addition in
about 85 CE when Matthew was written. Nevertheless
fifty-eight per cent voted favourably or half favourably.

Perhaps the next logical step ('pray continuously') in this
thought development is that the whole of life should be a
prayer process, being aware that each person with whom
we have daily contact has innately, as part of their being, a
spiritual dimension, even though at times it may be hard
to discern. I am reminded of a story, a parable really;
its source I have long since forgotten. A certain person
died and went to heaven but, even though he searched
the heavenly streets and mansions assiduously, he found
no-one. In despair he entered a mansion and sat down.
By and by a man came in and sat down opposite him.
'Where is everyone?' the recent arrival exclaimed. 'You
and I are the only ones here,' the man explained. 'And who
are you?' The man replied, 'I am Jesus. You see, everyone
with whom you came in contact with on earth was me!'

The corollary of this 'parable' is equally pertinent, maybe
even more pertinent lest we should be constantly patting
ourselves on the back and adding up our Brownie points.
Any good we do is not of our own doing but from an
innermost spiritual prompting, so to speak; and not in

any way expecting reciprocation or 'afterlife' rewards, as the reward is the act itself. Heaven is here and now!

One further point needs to be added here. Assuming that each of us is in possession of this 'divine' spirit and is a co-worker with it, it follows that what happens to us and what choices we make happens to God himself – he is with us as we move along this evolutionary parthway – neither party moving along a pre-ordained path. What happens to the world happens to God. Is that thought too hard to swallow? Maybe.

A useful contribution in a similar vein but extending the debate to our responsibility to life is introduced by that marvellous Jewish philosopher, Viktor Frankl, whose philosophies of life were moulded in the Nazi concentration camps where he lost his father, mother, brother and his wife when they were sent to the gas ovens:

...it did not really matter what we expected from life, but rather what life expected from us. We needed to stop asking about the meaning of life, and instead to think of ourselves as those who were being questioned by life – daily and hourly. Our answer must consist, not of talk and meditation, but in right action and in right conduct. Life ultimately means taking responsibility to find the right answer to its problems and to fulfil the tasks which it constantly sets for each individual...These tasks, and therefore the meaning of life, differ from man to man, and from moment to moment... and there is only one right answer to the problem posed by the situation at hand.[5]

One of the attractions of the formal church is that it guarantees life after death. The first unambiguous reference to an afterlife occurs in the last chapter of Daniel, seen by most scholars as the latest document of the Hebrew Bible, written around 165 BCE.

If one is baptised and participates regularly in the Mass or takes Communion one can by and large be reassured that one's place in the afterlife is assured, with one's name appearing boldly in the Book of Life. What security, what an insurance policy that is! My belief is that Jesus' teaching was not at all about any afterlife but about heaven being found here on earth and how to achieve this state. Most often in the gospels when the afterlife is mentioned, the subject is brought up by somebody else. It seems to me that Jesus himself was not very much concerned with life beyond death.[6]

The pinnacle of humanity then is to serve one's fellow man to the best of one's ability and to face one's last day with no regrets but with the satisfaction of having done one's best in this imperfect world and to acknowledge how fortunate one has been to have been granted such an experience.

What more should one expect at the end of life? The prospect of spending eternity singing hymns and luxuriating with some of the most disagreeable ponces one has ever come across is not appealing. The American Southern Baptist evangelist Billy Graham thought he might find golf courses in Heaven.[7] Would his swing be any better? If so, then the whole golfing *raison d'etre* would be defeated!

How much better is eternal sleep – dying with the gratitude that one has been granted the opportunity of participating in a lifetime of challenges, experiences and love. What extraordinary arrogance man displays to think that the Master of the Universe would endanger Himself by perpetuating man's miserable existence in a higher realm and run the risk of being told by the church hierarchy that the cosmos should head off in a different direction! And yet it remains a mystery, just as it should.

One final thought follows this scenario now set in place. If the spirit of the cosmos is present in creation, and in each of us as individuals, then at death this spirit returns to the source from whence it came and this part of us, at least, will abide forever stripped, of course, of our individual genetic dispositions, so the Bhuddists tell us.

Rex Hunt and John Smith are Australian Uniting Church pastors and members of the progressive Jesus Seminar who write:

...rather than a God 'out there' who can intervene and change the course of events, God has become for many progressives an 'inner voice', a 'presence within the human consciousness' that underpins life and enables humans to live well, justly and compassionately. Jesus puts a human face to such a divine presence...[8]

I am reminded of a remark made by my boss, Sir Rupert Magarey, at the end of his long and distinguished career as a surgeon, a remark made just before his retirement from The Queen Elizabeth Hospital in Adelaide: 'Well, Ross, all these difficult problems I shall happily pass on to the next man and he can bear the load.'

New Zealand teacher and theologian Lloyd Geering quotes Harvard Divinity School professor Gordon Kaulfman:

To believe in God is to commit oneself to a particular way of ordering one's life and action. It is to devote oneself to working towards a fully humane world within the ecological constraints here on planet Earth, while standing in piety and awe before the profound mysteries of existence.[9]

A similar thought was expressed by Albert Einstein, in his essay The World as I see it. Who better to have the last word than the greatest Jewish mind since Jesus!

How strange is the lot of mortals! Each of us is here for a brief sojourn; for what purpose he knows not, though he sometimes thinks he senses it. But without deeper reflection one knows from daily life that one exists for other people – first of all for those upon whose smiles and well-being our own happiness is wholly dependent, and then for the many, unknown to us, to whose destinies we are bound by the ties of sympathy. A hundred times every day I remind myself that my inner and outer life are based on the labours of other men, living and dead, and that I must exert myself in order to give in the same measure as I have received and am still receiving...

I have never looked upon ease and happiness as ends in themselves – this critical basis I call the ideal of a pigsty. The ideals that have lighted my way, and time after time have given me courage to face life cheerfully, have been Kindness, Beauty, and Truth...The trite objects of human efforts – possessions, outward success, luxury – have always seemed to me contemptible.

...The Jewish scriptures admirably illustrate the development from the religion of fear to moral religion, which is continued in the New Testament ...The development from a religion of fear to moral religion is a great step in a nation's life.

... But there is a third state of religious experience ...which I will call cosmic religious feeling. It is very difficult to explain this feeling to anyone who is entirely without it, especially as there is no anthropomorphic conception of God corresponding to it. [10]

The individual feels the nothingness of human desires and aims and the sublimity and marvellous order which reveal themselves both in nature and the world of thought. He looks upon individual existence as a sort of prison and wants to experience the universe as a single significant whole. The beginnings of cosmic religious feeling already appear in earlier stages of development, for example in many of the psalms of David and in some of the Prophets. Buddhism contains a much stronger element of it.

The religious geniuses of all ages have been distinguished by this kind of religious feeling, which knows no dogma and no God conceived in man's image; so there can be no Church whose central teachings are based on it. Hence it is precisely among the heretics of every age that we find men who were filled with the highest kind of religious feeling and were regarded by their contemporaries as atheists, sometimes also as saints. Looked at in this light, men like Democretus, Francis of Assisi, and Spinoza are closely akin to one another.

How can cosmic religious feeling be communicated from one person to another, if it can give rise to no definite notion of a God and no theology? In my view, it is the most important function of art and science to awaken this feeling and keep it alive in those who are capable of it.

...A man's ethical behaviour should be based effectually on sympathy, education, and social ties; no religious basis is necessary. Man indeed would be in a poor way if he had to be restrained by fear of punishment and hope of reward after death.[11]

And finally, Einstein on 'the religiousness' of science:

You will hardly find one among the profounder sort of scientific minds without a peculiar religious feeling of his own. But it is different from the religion of the naïve man. For the latter God is a being from whose care one hopes to benefit and whose punishment one fears; a sublimation of a feeling similar to that of a child for its father, a being to whom one stands to some extent in a personal relation, however deeply it may be tinged with awe.

But the scientist is possessed by the sense of universal causation. The future, to him, is every whit as necessary and determined as the past. There is nothing divine about morality, it is a purely human affair. His religious feeling takes the form of a rapturous amazement at the harmony of natural law, which reveals an intelligence of such superiority that, compared with it, all the systematic thinking and acting of human beings is an utterly insignificant reflection. This feeling is the guiding principle of his life and work, in so far as he succeeds in keeping himself from the shackles of selfish desire. It is beyond question closely akin to that which has possessed the religious geniuses of all ages. [12]

NOTES

1. Christina Rossetti, Who has seen the wind?, at http://www.poetryfoundation.org/poem/171952. Accessed 26 May 2013.

2. Susan Bridle, 'Comprehensive compassion: An Interview with Brian Swimme', What is enlightenment? Magazine, Issue 19 Spring-Summer 2001. Online at http://thegreatstory.org/SwimmeWIE.pdf. Accessed 26 May 2013.

3. Charles W. Hedrick, When faith meets reason, Polebridge Press, Salem, 2008, p. 21.

4. Robert Funk, The Five gospels: What did Jesus really say? Harper One, San Francisco, 1993, p. 148.

5. Viktor Frankl, Man's search for meaning, Beacon Press, Boston, 2006, p. 77.

6. Marcus Borg devotes a sement of his book to this topic in Speaking Christian, Harper One, San Francisco, 2001, pp. 197-201.

7. In a 1994 interview with Life Magazine, Billy Graham was asked if there would be golf courses in heaven. "If they're necessary for our happiness," he replied, "They'll be there." At the time of publication, Billy Graham is aged 94.

8. Rex A. E. Hunt & John W. H. Smith, (Ed.) Why weren't we told? A Handbook on progressive Christianity, Polebridge Press, Salem, 2013, p. 37.

9. Robert Jones, God, Galileo and Gerring: A Faith for the twenty-first century, Polebridge Press, Salem, 2005, p. 163.

10. Anthropomorphic: the attribution of human form or personality to God.

11. Albert Einstein, Ideas and opinions, Ed. Carl Seelig, Bonazna Books, New York, 1954, pp. 8-11.

12. ibid.

18

Bibliography

Augustine, *De Libero Arbitrio,* trans. Dom Mark Pontifes, Newman Press, London, 1955.

Barnett, Paul, *The Birth of Christianity: The First Twenty Years,* Wm B. Eerdmans Publishing Co., Grand Rapids, 2005.

Beutner, Edward F. (ed.), *Listening to the parables of Jesus,* Polebridge Press, Salem, 2007.

Bonhoeffer, Dietrich, *Letters and papers from prison,* Fontana Books, London, 1959.

Bonhoeffer, Dietrich, *No rusty swords,* The Fontana Library, London, 1970.

Borg, Marcus J. and Crossan, John Dominic, *The First Christmas,* Harper Collins, New York, 2007.

Borg, Marcus J. and Crossan, John Dominic, *The Last week,* Harper Collins, New York, 2006.

Borg, Marcus J. and Crossan, John Dominic, *The First Paul*, Harper Collins, New York, 2009.

Borg, Marcus J. and Wright, N. T., *The Meaning of Jesus,* Harper Collins, New York, 2000.

Borg, Marcus J., *Meeting Jesus again for the first time*, Harper Collins, New York, 1995.

Borg, Marcus J., *Speaking Christian,* Harper One, San Francisco, 2011.

Borg, Marcus J., *The Heart of Christianity*, Harper Collins, New York, 2003.

Borg, Marcus J., *The Lost Gospel Q*, Ulysses Press, Berkeley, 1999.

Calder, Nigel, *Einstein's universe*, Gramercy, London, 1988.

Craig, Edward, *Philosophy*, Sterling Publishing Company, New York, 2009. Online at books.google.com.au/books?isbn=140276877X. Accessed 22 May 2013.

Craig, Edward, *Philosophy: A Very short introduction,* Oxford University Press, London, 2002.

Crossan, John Dominic, *Jesus: A Revolutionary biography*, Harper Collins, New York, 1995.

Crossan, John Dominic and Watts, Richard G. (eds) *Who*

is Jesus?, Harper Collins/Westminster John Knox Press, Louisvile, 1996.

Crotty, Robert, *The Jesus question: the historical search,* Harper Collins, London, 1996.

Crotty, Robert, *Three revolutions: three drastic changes in interpreting the Bible*, ATF Theology Press, Adelaide, 2012.

Cupitt, Don, *The Future of the Christian tradition,* Polebridge Press, Salem, 2007.

Dahn, Felix, Ein Kampf um Rom, Breitopf & Härtel, 1876. Online at http://www.gutenberg.org/ebooks/31294. Accessed 24 May 2013.

Darwin, Charles, *The Origin of species,* 1859. Online at http://talkorigins.org/faqs/origin/chapter6.html. Accessessed 16 April 2013.

Dawkins, Richard, *The God delusion*, Bantam Books, London, 2006.

Descartes, Rene *Discourse on the method of rightly using one's reason and of using truth in the sciences,* 1637. Online at http://www.gutenberg.org/ebooks/59. Accessed 20 May 2012.

Ebert, John David, *Twilight of the clockwork God: conversations on science and spirituality at the end of an age,* Council Oak Books, Tulsa, 1999.

Einstein, Albert and Seelig Carl (ed.), *Ideas and Opinions*, Bonzana Books, New York, 1954.

Epstein, Isidore, *Judaism*, Penguin, New York, 1959.

Frankl, Viktor, *Man's search for meaning*, Beacon Press, Boston, 2006.

Funk, Robert W. (ed.), The Acts of Jesus, Polebridge Press, Salem, 1998.

Good, Jack, *The Dishonest Church*, Rising Star Press, Bend, 2003.

Hartshorne, Charles, *Omnipotence and Other Theological Mistakes*, Suny Press, New York, 1984.

Hawking, Stephen, *A Brief history of time,* Bantam Books, New York, 1988.

Hawking, Stephen, *Black Holes, Baby Universes and Other Essays*, Transworld, London, 1993.

Hedrick, Charles W.; Funk, Robert W.; Jackson, Glenna S.; Leaves, Nigel; Price, Robert M.; Laughlin, Paul Alan; Robinson, James M.; Smith, Mahlon H,; Weedon, Theodore J.; Wink, Walter; Galston, David; Middleton, Darren J. N.; Elliott, Susan M.; Talsick, Hal and Hedrick, Charles W. (ed.), *When faith meets reason*, Polebridge Press, Salem, 2008.

Hobsbawm, Eric, *On history,* Abacus, London, 1998.

Holloway, Richard, *Leaving Alexandria,* The Text Publishing Company, Melbourne, 2012.

Hume, David, *Enquiries concerning human understanding,* (ed.) L. A. Selby-Bigge, 3rd edition revised P. H. Nidditch, Clarendon Press, Oxford, 1975.

Hunt, Rex A. E. and Smith, W. H., *Why Weren't We Told?,* Polebridge Press, Salem, 2013.

Jones, Malcolm V. and Terry, Garth M., *New essays on Dostoyevsky, Cambridge University Press, Cambridge, 1983.*

Joy, Charles (ed.), *Albert Schweitzer, An Anthology,* A. & C. Black, London, 1952.

Kyokai, Bukkyo Dendo, *The Teaching of Buddha,* Kosaido, Tokyo, 2004.

Laertius, Diogenes, *Lives of the eminent philosophers,* Harvard University Press, Boston, 1972.

Lewis, C. S., *Mere Christianity,* Harper Collins, New York, 2002.

Livingstone, Gordon, *Too soon old, too late smart,* Da Capo Press, Cambridge, 2004.

Mack, Burton L., *Who wrote the New Testament?,* Harper Collins, New York, 1995.

Manning, Russell Re, *30-Second religion*, Sterling, New York, 2011.

Marx, Karl and Engel, Frederich, *The Communist Manifesto*, Penguin, London, 2004. Online at http://www.gutenberg.org/ebooks/61. Accessed 22 May 2013.

Mason, J. M. (ed. and trans.), *The Complete letters of Sigmund Freud to Wilhelm Fliess,* Harvard University Press, Cambridge, 1985.

Middleton, Darren J. N., *When faith meets religion,* Polebridge Press, Salem, 2008.

Miller, Robert J. (ed.), *The Future of the Christian tradition*, Polebridge Press, Salem, 2007.

Moloney, Francis J., *The Living Voice of the Gospel*, John Garrett Publishing, Melbourne, 2006.

Owen, David, *Nietzsche's Geneaology of Morality,* McGill Queens Univ., Montreal, 2007.

Phipps, Carter, 'A new dawn for cosmology: an interview with James Gardner', *Enlighten Next Magazine,* Issue 19 Spring Summer 2001. Online at http://www.enlightenmentnext.org/magazine/j33/gardner.asp. Accessed 16 April 2013.

Phipps, Carter, *Evolutionaries: unlocking the spiritual and cultural potential of science's greatest idea,* Harper Perennial, New York, 2012.

Plato, *The Last days of Socrates,* (ed.) Harrold Tarrant (trans.) High Tredennick, Penguin Books, London, 2003.

Pope Benedict XVI, *Easter address 2011.* Online at http://www.vatican.va/holy_father/benedict_xvi/messages/urbi/documents/ht_ben-xvi_mes_20110424_urbi-easter_en.html. Accessed 16 April 2013.

Ratzinger, Joseph, *Jesus of Nazareth,* Bloomsbury, London, 2007.

Sagan, Carl, *Cosmos,* Macdonald Futura Publishers, London, 1980.

Sanguin, Bruce, *Darwin, Divinity, and the Dance of the Cosmos: an ecological Christianity,* Wood Lake Publishing, Kelowna, 2007.

Schweiker, William, 'The Intellectual's responsibility and the abmiguity of the religions of the book, Part II: A Shared pattern of moral conviction', *Sightings,* University of Chicago, 24 October 2001.

Schweitzer, Albert, *The Quest for the Historical Jesus,* A. & C. Black Ltd, London, 1910.

Scott, Bernard Brandon (ed.), *Finding the Historical Jesus,* Polebridge Press, Salem, 2008.

Scott, Bernard Brandon (ed.), *Jesus Reconsidered*, Polebridge Press, Salem, 2007.

Solomon, Norman, *Judaism: A very short introduction*, Oxford University Press, London, 1996.

Spong, John Shelby, *A New Christianity for a New World*, Harper Collins, London, 2001.

Spong, John Shelby, *Born of a woman*, Harper Collins, New York, 1992.

Spong, John Shelby, *Jesus for the non religious*, Harper Collins, New York, 2007.

Spong, John Shelby, *Liberating the Gospels*, Harper Collins, New York, 1997.

Spong, John Shelby, *Resurrection: myth or reality*, Harper Collins, New York, 1995.

Spong, John Shelby, *Resuscitating the Bible from fundamentalism*, Harper Collins, New York, 1991.

Spong, John Shelby, *The Sins of scripture*, Harper Collins, New York, 2005.

Spong, John Shelby; Borg, Marcus; Funk, Robert W.; Crossan, John Dominic; King, Karen; Geering, Lloyd; Luedemann, Gerd; Sheehan, Thomas and Wink, Walter, *The Once and future Jesus*, Polebridge Press, Salem, 2001.

Spong, John Shelby; Borg, Marcus; Funk, Robert W.; Crossan, John Dominic; King, Karen; Geering, Lloyd; Luedemann, Gerd; Sheehan, Thomas and Wink, Walter, *What did Jesus really say?*, Harper Collins, New York, 1997.

Tabor, James D., *The Jesus dynasty,* Harper Collins, New York, 2007.

Tacey, David, *The Spirituality revolution*, Harper Collins, New York, 2003.

Tacitus, Publius (or Gaius) Cornelius, *The Annals,* ACE 109 trans. Church, Alfred John and Brodribb, William Jackson. Online at http://clasics.nit.edu/Tacitus/annals.html. Accessed 22 May 2013.

Thakur, Biman Narayan, *Poetic plays of Sri Aurobino,* online at books.google.com.au/books?isbn=8172111819. Accessed 22 May 2013.

Tranquillus, Gaius Suetonius, *Lives of the Caesars*: *Claudius,* AD 121 (also translated as *Lives of the Twelve Caesars*). Online at http://www.gutenberg.org/ebooks/6390. Accessed 22 May 2013.

Tranquillus, Gaius Suetonius, *Lives of the Caesars*: *Nero,* AD 121 (also translated as *Lives of the Twelve Caesars*). Online at http://www.gutenberg.org/ebooks/6391. Accessed 22 May 2013.

Vernon, Mark, *Science, religion and the meaning of life*, Palgrave Macmillan, London, 2007.

Vosper, Gretta, *With or without God*, Harper Perennial, New York, 2009.

Watson, Peter, *Ideas: A History from Fire to Freud*, Phoenix, London, 2006.

West, Morris, *A View from the ridge*, Harper Collins, New York, 1996.

Wetherill, Tim, 'Cosmic Time Machine', *ScienceWise Magazine*, Autumn 2010. Online at http://sciencewise.anu.edu.au/articles/moon%20rock. Accessed 6 June 2011.

Woodhead, Linda, *Christianity: A Very short introduction*, Oxford University Press, London, 2004.

Yutang, Lin, *The Importance of Living*, William Heinemann Ltd., London, 1938.